Bricks in a Pebble Sauce:
Francine's Favorite French Family Recipes and Memories

Francine Martinie Chough

BRICKS IN A PEBBLE SAUCE: FRANCINE'S FAVORITE FRENCH FAMILY RECIPES AND MEMORIES

Copyright © 2022 by Francine Martinie Chough. All rights reserved. Printed in the United States of America.

No parts of this book may be used, copied, or reproduced in any matter without the written permission of the author.

ISBN: 978-0-578-29718-7

First edition: July 1, 2022

Photographs and Illustrations

Unless indicated the photographs for this book are my own. I am deeply thankful for the additional contribution of images, in particular French artist Laurence Bonfils the founder of La Cité créative, a creative and teaching atelier in Annecy, France for providing her beautiful illustrations.

Marie Marchat (cover, 266)

Jean Chough (back cover, 263)

Laurence Bonfils (2, 6, 10, 74, 82, 85, 112, 115, 135, 154, 252, 262, 265)

Katharine Jensen (106, 234, 236)

Craig Knott (269)

Fabienne Martinie (270)

Michael Moore (39, 163, 191, layout design)

Sherri Roberts (126)

Foreword

Celebrations of foods and traditions are my favorite themes and passions. Through Francine's family recipes and delightful stories, I was transported back to memories of my grandparents with the aromas of food always simmering on the corner of the cooking range. Grand Mère's *crème renversée au caramel* and *confitures* were always waiting for us at each visit. The exquisite and delicate white asparagus proudly harvested from Grand Père's garden every springtime, and the *mousseline* sauce made of the fresh eggs from his *poulailler* and *crème fraiche* maturing long enough before being churned into butter would always be among our family's favorites.

Being raised in the sixties and seventies at the family bakery, I would wake up with the air filled with the smell of brioche and breads every morning on the way out to school. I have always considered myself privileged being surrounded with such epicurean talents. These years were still close enough from the privations from WW II that food, all food, was preciously prepared and revered. Nothing was wasted and the simplest ingredient would always find virtue in a delectable meal.

Merci Francine for creating this book and sharing the importance of family cooking traditions from France. Whenever I see a recipe attached with a family tradition and a story, it becomes a true celebration of life.

Bon Appétit!

Dominique Geulin, Meilleur Ouvrier de France
Chef owner Saint Honoré Boulangerie

Introduction

This book is an homage to my parents, the two towering influences that gave me my enthusiasm for family cooking, learning, and teaching.

As a teenager, I remember they attended Françoise Bernard cooking classes, a popular cooking writer and radio personality. From one of her classes, they came home with her book "Les recettes faciles"-"Easy recipes." A book I still have today. They also watched legendary three-star Michelin chef Raymond Oliver's television show called "Art et magie de la cuisine" in the '60s to learn how to make all kinds of special dishes. This is where my father learned to master soufflés.

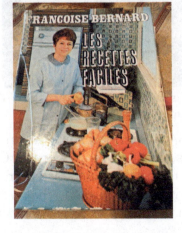

As a couple, they were partners in the kitchen long before their time. My mom, "Mamie Gisèle" would prepare the appetizers, soups, salads, and main courses. She would use a cookbook from 1934 "La Véritable Cuisine de Famille par Tante Marie", the same copy I now have. It is unlike any cookbook you see today. There are no measurements or oven temperature, no technique; it is as if French homemakers knew exactly how to cook in certain quantities without measuring or timing anything.

My mom would cook by feel. If we kids wanted to peek into the pots on the stove to see what was cooking, just before lunch, she would say, *"On mange des briques à la sauce caillou"* —"We are going to eat bricks in a pebble sauce"!!!

My dad, being a baker's son and a baker's brother-in-law liked exactness, his specialty was making desserts on the weekend. My dad loved to bake cakes, clafoutis, crepes, cheese soufflés, Grand Marnier soufflés, mousses, fruit tarts and bread puddings among other things. He would be collecting various recipes. I found so many versions of chocolate cake with different proportions that I made my own inspired by his comments.

On most Sundays, when they did not feel like cooking, my dad would tell my mom that he would make reservations in a traditional local gourmet restaurant in a remote village for lunch. So, I have tried the best food of Burgundy, where I grew up!

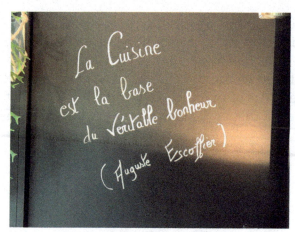

"Cooking is the basis of true joy."
Auguste Escoffier

In the mid-eighties, while in the USA, I attended some Asian cooking classes taught by Kary Arimoto-Mercer. As I learned more Korean, Chinese, and Japanese cooking from her, we struck a friendship and started an "East Meets West" cooking course. When she moved away, I continued what was natural for me and I started a class called "Easy French Cooking" for Americans who were intimidated by French cooking.

I have always loved cooking. It is very therapeutic for me. It channels my creative energy by making new dishes or improving existing ones. For me, cooking for someone is to give my heart, it is a labor of love, and an act of love. I appreciate the fact that you can use all your senses. Over the years, I have developed a greater patience, a love for others and a craving to prepare simpler, classical, and seasonal French dishes that I humbly share with family and friends. What a pleasure to see someone enjoy what you have prepared!

You can learn a lot about a country by cooking or eating its food. Family food represents the history of that family and their culture. Many dishes have roots in history, geography, religion, and local traditions. Our daughter's godmother, Consuelo Casey, used to say: "If everyone from different countries would gather around a table to eat each other's foods, there would be no wars."

As an immigrant from France to the USA in the late '70s, French food was always for me a source of comfort and security in the new world, when sometimes I was not familiar about my new adopted culture and cuisine. French family cooking was something I could fall back onto when I was homesick.

I had a good guinea pig at home to try my food: my husband Jean, originally from South Korea, who happened to enjoy all kinds of food but especially French food! When our daughter Natacha came along, she was also enrolled as a guinea pig, and was always willing to try my creations. For me, it is a way of transmitting my heritage and culture to our daughter. Her husband Craig has been enrolled as a food taster now! They are both great cooks, avid foodies, gourmets and willing to try most of my French dishes.

"Cooking is a form of art, a gift to share."
Oprah Winfrey

How to use this Cookbook

As mentioned in the introduction, my mom, Mamie Gisèle, was familiar with "La Véritable Cuisine de Famille par Tante Marie"- "True Family Cooking by Aunt Marie." It dates to 1934 and can be found today in new versions. It was unlike the detailed step-by-step cookbooks of today. Tante Marie assumed her readers had a functional knowledge of how to cook. There was no indication that she used quantities, measurements, or specific temperature when she prepared something. To season a dish, "taste it and adjust seasonings." For another recipe, "You put the roast in a warm oven" were some of her directions. It was up to you to watch it and know when it was fully cooked! It assumed with repetition, trial, and error those skills and intuitions would develop. This was how my mom cooked, by feel and by being creative.

This cookbook sits between the world of Tante Marie, and the detailed instruction manual approach of some cookbooks today. I list ingredients in both volumes and weights since many cooks today use digital kitchen scales for ease and precision. I list the equipment needed and give simple clear instructions for each recipe adding temperatures and quantities when critical and important. As with all recipes—read thoroughly before you begin.

This book is a guide to my French family's home recipes. It is not a comprehensive French cookbook. This is not a cookbook for a novice or someone who is not familiar with cooking. It assumes a basic knowledge of cooking.

I have used terms that are familiar to me, like pâte à choux, puff pastry, shortbread, tempering chocolate, roux, a water bath, a double boiler for example. If they are unfamiliar to you, a quick search of the internet will provide clarification and, if necessary, detailed instruction.

When I mention an ingredient like a lemon, lemons come in varied sizes and give a different amount of juice: between 4 and 8 tablespoons, average. If you see a medium onion and have a large one, adjust and use less. Same thing when making an apple tart that calls for large apples and you only have small ones. Line up the slices on your tart and if you need one more, go ahead, cut an extra one.

The one drawback to overly prescriptive cookbooks is while they may make cooks feel more secure, they can also make them timid. And timid is a word that would never describe the French home cook…. Particularly Mamie Gisèle!

Trust yourself, be creative, and enjoy the experience!

Bonne cuisine!

Table of Contents

Home Cooking in France 2

Essentials for a French Pantry 6

Sauces 8

Appetizers & Salads 20

Soups 64

Quick Meals 78

Main Dishes 92

Side Dishes 138

Cheese 152

Desserts 158

Holiday Dishes 222

Drinks 250

Seasonal Menu Ideas 260

Shopping for Food According to Mamie Gisèle 262

At the French Table 265

Tips and Hacks 267

Acknowledgements 269

Home Cooking in France

In the southern region of France near where my parents grew up there is a motto *bien manger c'est notre nature* – "Eating well is in our nature."

When we were kids, my mom would tell us what she planned to prepare for lunch. We would salivate in anticipation of the meal to come. Invariably she would return from the market and prepare something different according to what she found that day. While the idea of eating what is seasonal, local, and fresh is beginning to take hold in the United States, it has always been the basis of eating well in France.

What constitutes seasonal, local, and fresh is the result of the geographic and climatic diversity of France. In an area about the size of Texas, the cuisines of the north and the south, the east and the west are shaped by the unique ingredients of their region. The mountainous areas of the Alps in the east, and the Pyrenees in the south are as different from one another as the coastal provinces of Normandy and Brittany on the English Channel are from the Mediterranean cities and towns of Provence. To say nothing of the culinary differences of cosmopolitan cities and rural countryside.

Most of northern France uses butter as its principal fat while the southern preference is olive oil. The west coast and the southern coast make use of all the seafood found in their oceans and seas. The flavors of Normandy in the northwest rely on cream and butter while the east regions of Burgundy, Alsace and the Southwest region of Bordeaux often feature wine. The Alps regions like Savoie and Haute-Savoie use a lot of cheese while along the Mediterranean coast in addition to olive oil, you will find tomatoes and garlic as in Italian cuisine. Depending on where you are from, the same food may have different names: in the northern part of France, we eat *pain au chocolat* for breakfast, but if you are from the south, you would eat a *chocolatine*.

Local, seasonal products are to be had, by virtue of year-round outdoor markets in every town or city. When planning menus and shopping, the season is always your guide. If the season for strawberries is finished, then we eat raspberries and so on throughout the year. There is always an anticipation of when the asparagus or the cherries are coming in season. We do not eat strawberries in winter. That is the time for chestnuts, in the spring we eat asparagus, in summer we eat peaches, in the fall we eat mushrooms. In the country, if it is the season to kill the pig or the calves, then that meat is either eaten at that specific season or preserved for later. And with everything there was always bread!

Bread has been the staple in France for a long time although now, the younger generations eat less bread. In our home, wasting bread was a particular sin! Bread was sacred. It was a crime to throw bread away and it would bring you bad luck. My mom, who was from the Greatest Generation, was horrified if she saw baguettes in the garbage cans on the street. In French, we have an expression *gagner son pain* meaning "to earn their bread." My mom used to say if someone threw bread away it meant they did not know how to earn a living.

In the countryside, where my parents grew up, if there was nothing much to eat, you could always eat bread with a soup or with cheese. If the soup was not hardy enough, they would add torn pieces of bread. If there was soup leftover, they would dilute it in the plate with red wine for a *chabrot* an expression meaning to finish off the soup with red wine. If there was bread left over, we would make *des pains dorés* or *du pain perdu* for dinner like French toast. We made breadcrumbs for the next *gratin* or to add to meatballs or stuffing. We use the stale bread cubes to dip in the *Fondue Savoyarde*. We would slice the baguette, brush it with olive oil and toast them to put on top of onion soup.

When we had too much bread leftover, my dad loved to make *le pudding*, a dessert made with milk, raisins, and sugar! He also liked to put *pain bis* – a country rye bread bought in the Limousin region—in his soup to thicken it.

In France, from 6:00 a.m. until 3:00 p.m. the boulangeries are open every day, even on Sundays. We like to buy fresh bread every day. On Mondays, most boulangeries are closed but there is always *a boulangerie de garde* (on duty boulangerie on Mondays) open on that day, just like there is *a pharmacie de garde* open on Sundays.

Given the care and attention to preparation, meals were never wasted. At our home, we tried to make use of the leftovers by creating a new dish, so we did not eat the same thing over and over. For example, if my mom made *soupe de légumes*, a vegetable soup, one day she would thin out half of it with broth for another dinner and add some pastinis, orzo, or vermicelli. If she made a roast, my dad would grind the meat the next day and make a *Hachis Parmentier*, cottage pie, stuffed tomatoes and potatoes, or stuffed mushrooms.

If Mamie Gisèle made mayonnaise and it was a flop, she would not throw it away. She started over with 1 egg yolk, a little vinegar and mustard and with a beater, trickle in the flopped mayo and then trickle some more oil at the end and the mayo was rescued. If she had too much mayo for a dish, she did not throw it away but place it in an airtight container in the fridge for a few days. If the eggs were fresh and preserved correctly in the fridge, it would be safe.

Growing up in Burgundy, there was a lot of wine and cheese around. When a bottle of wine was not finished or was not that good, Mamie Gisèle, used it in cooking instead of throwing it away. She would make *Boeuf bourguignon* or *Oeufs en meurette*.

If a cheese was getting dry because we did not eat it fast enough, it was grated and put on *Gratin Savoyard* or in *Macaroni au gratin*, the American favorite mac and cheese. If it were a creamy cheese, we would spread it on top of potatoes, mix it in a *Purée*, or melt it under the broiler and dip fresh vegetables in it.

For breakfast, we ate *tartines*—a slice of bread and butter with jam or cheese accompanied by either a *café au lait*, *café noir*, or *chocolat chaud*— hot chocolate. Unless we got in trouble in which case, we were only allowed stale bread to put in our morning drink. *Croissants* were reserved for the weekend. Nowadays many younger families have adopted British or American type cereals. Some also eat Muesli in the eastern part of France.

In the countryside, the main meal is lunch, the biggest meal of the day and would typically be at least three or four courses: an appetizer like a cucumber salad, or a pâté, a main course of meat and a vegetable, cheese and a dessert like some fruit, or a fruit tart. We would eat around 12:00/12:30 p.m.. As a first course, you might have a tomato salad, a potato salad, a grated carrot salad, a cucumber salad, or a red beets salad. The French do not eat a green salad as a first course, it is always served after the main course to cleanse your palate before the cheese course. And always with homemade salad dressing. A country evening meal would be much lighter consisting of a soup, or an omelet, or even yogurt or cheeses and fruit. Of course, we eat bread with all these. And no butter on the bread!

In the city, people eat a quick lunch *sur le pouce*—literally "on the thumb" or "on the run" and eat a more substantial meal for dinner. Lunch is typically eaten between 12 and 1:00 p.m.. If you worked in the city, it would be a *jambon-beurre*—a baguette with butter, ham, and cheese—consumed on the run. Or, if you dined at a bistro it might consist of a *croque-monsieur* or the *plat du jour*, the special dish the bistro is serving that day. The main meal is in the evening and is served at

7:00-7:30 p.m. or even 8:00 p.m.. No restaurants would be open before that hour! At home, we would observe the same schedule, which meant often some families have a *goûter*, an afternoon snack—for the children like a *pain au chocolat* or a *pain aux raisins*. Seniors would have tea or coffee in the afternoon with some biscuits.

For birthdays, anniversaries, communions, baptisms and weddings or life celebration events, we could spend 2 to 3 hours at the table with family members or friends. The meal could be 6 to 7 courses, but the portions are quite small and very manageable. Often, there would be a pause in the middle of the meal to help you digest. You would have a sorbet with some local alcohol, or just a swigger of Calvados (Apple Jack, a specialty liquor from Normandy) called *le trou normand* a tradition from Normandy, a good reason to clean your insides for the next dish. All these banquets would have a variety of wines: aperitifs, whites, reds, rosés, Champagne, digestifs! Better not drive on the roads on those weekends!

Food is especially important in France and the relationship French people have with food defines much of its culture and character. We are always planning on what the next meal is going to be. Remember the portions are small so you can have that variety of courses. My mom used to say *on creuse sa tombe avec ses dents*, "you dig your grave with your teeth" so she was careful to serve healthy and smaller meals. We enjoy all the flavors each region of France has to offer, and we love to spend time preparing and sharing meals, especially on the weekend or for special occasions. It is said that some people eat to live. But for most French people it is, *nous vivons pour manger*... "We live to eat!"

"Good food, good wines, good companions are the best of therapies."

Essentials for a French Pantry

CONDIMENTS

- ☐ Olive oil—both an extra virgin for dressing and finishing and a good pure less expensive one for cooking. Sunflower oil is often used in areas outside of Provence.
- ☐ Red or white wine vinegars.
- ☐ Prepared Dijon mustard like Maille, Amora, Grey Poupon, Pommery or Fallot.
- ☐ Salt, preferably sea salt, and peppercorns.

VEGETABLES

- ☐ Shallots and garlic
- ☐ Onion, celery, and carrots
- ☐ Tomatoes
- ☐ Dried or fresh mushrooms

DAIRY

- ☐ Milk, cream, or crème fraiche
- ☐ Butter both salted and unsalted

- ☐ Cheese preferably hard, shredded, and easy to melt like Gruyère, Comté.

MEAT (CHARCUTERIE) AND EGGS

- ☐ Jambon or ham
- ☐ Bacon
- ☐ Eggs

SPICES AND HERBS

- ☐ Piment d'Espelette
- ☐ Nutmeg
- ☐ Herbes de Provence, which is a blend of thyme, oregano, rosemary and sometimes savory
- ☐ Bouquet garni which is a sprig of parsley, a sprig of thyme and a bay leaf bound together with string or twine

WINE, LIQUORS AND STOCKS

- ☐ Wine—red and white
- ☐ Stock—chicken, beef, or vegetable
- ☐ Grand Marnier, rum, kirsch

DRY

- ☐ All-purpose flour   American flour has more gluten than French flour so you might want a variety depending on the recipe.
- ☐ Granulated sugar
- ☐ Confectioner's sugar
- ☐ Dark or bitter chocolate
- ☐ A variety of pasta, rice, lentils, beans

Sauces

What are the French Mother Sauces 10

Mayonnaise 10

Aioli 11

Tartar Sauce 11

Béchamel Sauce 12

Mornay Sauce 13

Soubise Sauce 13

Aurora Sauce 14

White Sauce 14

Hunter's Sauce 15

Maxine's Salmon Sauce 16

Vinaigrette Gisèle Martinie 18

What are the French Mother Sauces

The mother sauces are basic to French cuisine. Escoffier is the first chef to write about them. There are 5, 6 or 7 depending on whom you talk to.

By adding another ingredient to one of the basic sauces you can create an entirely different sauce for different dishes. For example, a béchamel sauce is made with a roux of hot butter and flour and when foaming you add cold milk. You add salt and pepper and there you have it! It is a basic sauce in French cuisine. You use it to make a cheese soufflé or macaroni and cheese.

If you add cheese to that sauce, it is called a mornay sauce. If you add onions, it is called a soubise sauce. If you add tomato paste, it is called aurora sauce. These are secondary sauces.

I have divided the mother sauces into two categories; emulsion sauces made with egg, oil or butter and roux based sauces made with butter and flour.

I am not covering all the sauces, only the ones my family and I use on a regular basis.

Serves as desired   Intermediate

Mayonnaise Sauce

This is an emulsion sauce so all ingredients should be at room temperature. Mayonnaise will be a flop if some ingredients are colder than others, the oil has been added too fast at the beginning, or if there is too much oil for the quantity of egg.

- 1 large egg yolk at room temperature
- ½ tablespoon Dijon mustard at room temperature
- ½ tablespoon white, cider, or wine vinegar
- Salt and pepper
- ⅓ to ½ cup extra virgin olive oil, safflower, peanut, or corn oil
- At the end: 1 teaspoon vinegar and 1 tablespoon boiling water

Needed

- Stand or handheld mixer or food processor
- Medium mixing bowl

1) Mix the first three ingredients beating at medium high speed.
2) When the mixture is smooth and well blended, add the oil in a trickle until the mayonnaise starts to thicken and take shape. Keep beating at high speed the whole time. At this point you can pour the oil in a bigger stream.
3) When the mayonnaise is set, you can add 1 teaspoon of vinegar and/or a teaspoon of boiling water to make the sauce lighter and hold better.
4) Add salt and pepper to taste.

Serve with cold meats like chicken, on sandwiches, with salads, cold fish, raw or blanched vegetables, deviled eggs.

Tips

If your mayonnaise failed, do not throw it away! Start over with an egg yolk, mustard and vinegar, salt and pepper and slowly trickle the failed mixture. If you need to add a little oil afterwards, go ahead.

Aioli Sauce

- 6 cloves of minced garlic

1) Add the minced garlic to the finished mayonnaise from above and mix well.

Serve with roasted vegetables or Bouillabaisse (when you finish eating the broth then you eat the fish with the aioli).

It can be used as a dip for blanched cauliflower, broccoli, green beans, carrots, steamed fish, potato salad.

Tartar Sauce

- 1 teaspoon vinegar
- 1 minced shallot
- 2 teaspoons capers
- 4 to 5 minced cornichons
- Parsley, chives, chervil, tarragon minced

1) Follow the mayonnaise directions and at the end, add vinegar, the shallot, capers, pickles, and the minced herbs. Mix well in the sauce.

This is a tangy sauce to serve with fried or broiled fish, cold meats or as a side sauce when you make a Fondue Burgundy Style (page112).

Béchamel Sauce

This is a roux-based sauce that uses milk. The main idea with all the flour-based sauces is to avoid lumps! Use a wire or a wooden whisk to avoid this. It will also thicken faster. It is also critical to have a cold liquid to pour in a hot fat/flour mixture.

- 2 tablespoons unsalted butter
- 2 tablespoons all-purpose flour
- Salt and pepper
- 1½ cup cold 2% or whole milk
- Grated nutmeg

Needed

- ➤ Medium saucepan
- ➤ Whisk

1) On medium heat, melt the butter. When sizzling, add the flour and cook a few seconds until foaming.
2) Pour the cold milk gradually and keep stirring with a whisk until the mixture starts to thicken.
3) Add salt and pepper and grated nutmeg.
4) The sauce can stay warm for a little while.

Serve hot over poached, or broiled fish, over chicken or pork, steamed vegetables, hard boiled eggs, macaroni, inside croque-monsieur.

Mornay Sauce

- ½ cup grated cheese

1) Make the béchamel sauce following the directions above.
2) When it is ready, add the grated cheese and salt and pepper depending how salty the cheese is.
3) The sauce can stay warm for a little while.

Particularly good when served with steamed cauliflower and potatoes, spinach, and macaroni.

Soubise Sauce

- 1 or 2 medium sliced, blanched, and sautéed onions

1) Make the béchamel sauce following the directions above.
2) When the béchamel sauce is ready, add the sautéed sliced onions, previ-

ously blanched 10 minutes to keep their white color, then sautéed 10 to 15 minutes in butter.

3) Add salt and pepper.
4) The sauce can stay warm for a little while. Before serving you can add a dollop of sour cream or crème fraiche.

Goes well on artichoke bottoms, white meats, steamed cauliflower and potatoes, spinach, and macaroni.

Aurora Sauce

- 1 tablespoon tomato paste at the last minute

1) Make the béchamel sauce following directions above.
2) When the échamel sauce is ready, add the tomato paste and mix well.

Serve over hard boiled eggs, steamed fish, white meats, steamed cauliflower, or broccoli.

White Sauce

This is a roux-based sauce that uses broth.

- 2 tablespoons unsalted butter
- 2 tablespoons all-purpose flour
- 1 cup ½ cold broth (chicken, fish broth, beef, or vegetable)
- Salt and pepper (If you use bouillon cubes and water do not add salt)

1) On low heat, melt the butter. When sizzling, add the flour and cook for a few seconds until foaming.
2) Pour the cold broth gradually as you are whisking. Pouring a cold liquid into a hot fat/flour mixture will usually prevent lumps from forming. Keep whisking until the mixture thickens.

3) Add salt and pepper after tasting.

Usually served with meat that is matched to the broth used. Sautéed mushrooms can be added.

Hunter's Sauce

A roux-based sauce that uses wine.

- ½ pound sliced button mushrooms (225 grams)
- 2 tablespoons unsalted butter
- 2 minced shallots
- 2 tablespoons flour
- ¾ cup white wine
- ¾ cup broth (chicken or beef)
- 2 tablespoons tomato paste
- 1 bouquet garni made from 1 bay leaf, 1 branch of thyme, 1 branch parsley tied with string to ease removal. Or use 1 teaspoon each of dried herbs.
- Salt and pepper

1) Sauté the sliced mushrooms with the shallots in butter until limp. Sprinkle with the flour all over. Mix well and cook a few seconds until foaming.

2) Add the wine gradually, stir in the tomato paste, then slowly add the cold broth. Whisk until thickened.

3) Add the bouquet garni and salt and pepper.

4) Cover and simmer for 15 minutes. Sprinkle parsley over your dish before serving.

Serve over sautéed meats, especially good with chicken pieces, filet mignon, veal chops, or rabbit pieces.

Maxine's Salmon Sauce

Sauce Maxine pour le saumon

Before moving to the USA, I have never eaten salmon as good as the ones prepared by Maxine Kopczynski. Maxine, her husband Kop, and their family used to go fishing in Alaska and Canada and bring back a bounty of Chinook and Coho. They were grilled on the barbecue and served with this warm sauce that my family has adopted and serves with salmon fillets. It has become a family classic!

Maxine has been known to substitute tarragon white wine vinegar for the white wine and it was just as delicious!

Yields 1 cup   Easy

- 1 stick of unsalted butter (113 grams)
- 2 cloves minced garlic
- 1 tablespoon soy sauce
- 1 tablespoon dry mustard
- ¼ to ⅓ cup dry white wine
- 2 ½ tablespoons ketchup

Needed

> Saucepan

1) Melt the butter with garlic in a saucepan.

2) Add the soy sauce and mustard. Mix well.

3) Add the wine and mix in the ketchup. Keep warm on low heat. Do not cook too long or the ingredients will separate

4) This can be refrigerated for a few days, reheat on low heat before serving.

Vinaigrette Gisèle Martinie

Makes enough for serving 4-6   Easy

- 1 clove garlic or 1 shallot minced
- ½ tablespoon Dijon mustard
- ½ tablespoon white, cider or wine vinegar
- 3 to 4 tablespoons olive, safflower, peanut or corn oil
- Salt and pepper to taste

Needed

- Bowl or a small dressing bottle
- Salad tongs

1) Mix the dressing in a bowl in the order given.
2) Pour over the salad and mix with salad tongs at the last minute since the dressing might burn the greens if left too long on the lettuce.

Tips

You can add herbs like Herbes de Provence, a chopped hard-boiled egg, Parmesan or Feta cheese, or anchovy for a different flavor.

I usually double, triple or quadruple this recipe so I can fill a bottle of dressing to have on hand for various salads or marinades. In that case, use as much as you want of mustard and one volume of vinegar for three or four of oil. If it is too tart for you add more oil.

It will keep for at least a week on the kitchen counter. If it has fresh garlic, refrigerate and bring to room temperature before serving.

Appetizers & Salads

Artichoke Bottoms Filled with Mixed Vegetable Salad 22

Asparagus with Mousseline Sauce 24

Vegetable Salad 27

Anchovy Butter 29

Canapés 30

Celeriac Salad 33

Greek Style Marinated Mushrooms 35

Eggs in Red Wine Sauce 37

Pâte à Choux 39

Cocktail Savory Little Choux 40

Gougères 42

Potato Salad with Chunky Tuna 44

Red Beets Salad 46

Grated Carrot Salad 48

Tomato Salad 50

Niçoise Salad 52

Cucumber Salad 54

Green Salad 56

Cheese Soufflé 58

Country Pâté 61

Artichoke Bottoms filled with Mixed Vegetable Salad
Fonds d'artichauts jardinière

This is a first course, fast to prepare, especially if you have last minute guests, using frozen or canned mixed vegetables, and canned artichoke bottoms. The assembly of this dish should take you only a few minutes.

Serves 6 to 8   Easy

Bottoms and filling

- ½ to 1 pound frozen or canned mixed vegetables including any of the following: carrots, peas, corn kernels, chopped green beans, white cannellini beans (225 to 450 grams)
- 1 can of well drained artichoke bottoms about 6 or 8
- 1 cup of shredded carrots mixed with vinaigrette or 4 to 6 lettuce leaves

Mayonnaise

- 1 large egg yolk at room temperature
- ½ tablespoon Dijon mustard at room temperature
- ½ tablespoon white, cider, or wine vinegar
- Salt and pepper
- ⅓ to ½ cup extra virgin olive oil, safflower, peanut, or corn oil
- At the end: 1 teaspoon vinegar and 1 tablespoon boiling water

Needed

- ➢ Stand mixer or food processor
- ➢ Serving platter

1) Mix the first four mayonnaise ingredients, while beating them, add the oil gradually in a trickle. The mixture will thicken (emulsify). If it fails to thicken you have added the oil too quickly. Start again by combining the first three ingredients in a new clean bowl. Mix thoroughly and then add the failed sauce in a slow trickle. The mayonnaise should emulsify then. Adjust salt and pepper if necessary.

2) Mix the mayonnaise with the vegetables and fill the artichoke bottoms.

3) Lay the artichoke bottoms on a bed of shredded carrots or lettuce mixed with Vinaigrette Gisèle Martinie page 18.

Tips

If you do not have time for homemade mayonnaise, you can use store bought but make sure it does not have sugar in it!

Asparagus with a Mousseline Sauce
Asperges sauce Mousseline

In my family, we loved to eat steamed asparagus as an appetizer with a sauce. When we did not have time to make a sauce, we would mix 1 or 2 tablespoons of Dijon mustard with 1 or 2 tablespoons of mayonnaise and a tablespoon of vinegar. Mix very well and there you have a "sauce rémoulade."

There are quite a few variations of mousseline sauce whether you want a cold sauce or a warm sauce. These are more elegant sauces for this dish. You could also try a hollandaise sauce.

Serves 4 to 6   Intermediate

- One large bunch of cleaned and trimmed green or white asparagus, about 32 asparagus

Needed

- 9x13 glass dish
- Paring knife
- Plastic wrap

1) Steam a bunch of asparagus in the microwave. Put the spears in a 9 by 13 glass dish with the tips facing each other. Cover with plastic wrap and make holes with a knife so the steam can escape. Cook for 3 minutes then rotate the dish and cook another 3 minutes. You can also blanch them in boiling water, in a stock pot, for about 5 minutes until cooked but still firm.

2) Let them rest on paper towel to drain so the water does not dilute the sauce.

Cold mousseline sauce
This is a mayonnaise with egg whites beaten stiff. All your ingredients should be at room temperature to be successful.

- 1 large egg yolk
- ½ tablespoon Dijon mustard
- 1 teaspoon cider, wine vinegar or lemon juice
- ⅓ to ½ cup of safflower oil or olive oil
- ½ teaspoon salt and ¼ teaspoon pepper
- 1 large egg white
- ⅛ teaspoon cream of tartar

Needed

- Stand mixer, handheld mixer, or a food processor
- Measuring spoons and cups
- 2 mixing bowls
- Spatula

1) In a mixing bowl, beat the egg yolk, Dijon mustard and the vinegar at high speed. When the mixture is getting thick, add the oil in a trickle, very slowly until the mayonnaise takes shape.
When it is thick like a mayonnaise, add salt and pepper to taste.

2) In a clean mixing bowl, beat the egg whites at high speed. When they look foaming, add the cream of tartar, and beat faster until they become firm.

3) Fold ⅓ of the egg whites at a time, in the mayonnaise, with a spatula and continue until everything is incorporated.

4) Serve cold over the cooked asparagus.

Warm mousseline sauce
This sauce can be served warm or lukewarm.

- 2 large egg yolks
- 2 ¾ tablespoons water
- A few drops of lemon juice or cider vinegar
- Salt and pepper
- 7 tablespoons cubed unsalted butter (100 grams)
- 2 tablespoons whipped cream

Needed

- Small saucepan
- Whisk
- Measuring spoons

1) On low heat, put the egg yolks in a pan with the water, salt and pepper, and a few drops of lemon juice. Do not burn the eggs. Use a whisk until the mixture thickens and sticks to the whisk.
2) Off the heat, add the butter slowly, tablespoon by tablespoon so it melts gradually.
3) When the sauce is smooth and ready, add the whipped cream. Mix until smooth. Taste and adjust seasoning.
4) Serve warm over the cooked asparagus.

Tips

You will have some leftover sauces. You can keep them in an airtight container in the fridge for several days. Mix well if the sauce separates.

These two variations of mousseline sauce are also good over poached or steamed fish, seafood and other steamed vegetables like artichokes, green beans, and broccoli.

Vegetable Salad

Assiette de crudités

This was a favorite of my family in France as a first course year-round or as a main course in summer when you want a light and cool meal.

You can also make a 3 ways crudités salad using beet salad, grated carrots, and sliced cucumber or tomato salad. Very colorful and refreshing. We used to have that regularly in the summer at my parents' house.

Serves 4 to 6   Easy

- 1 head of butter lettuce
- 2 or 3 peeled and sliced tomatoes
- 2 or 3 hard-boiled eggs sliced or halved
- 1 can of sardines in oil or a can of tuna in oil

Vinaigrette

- 1 to 2 cloves garlic minced
- ½ tablespoon Dijon mustard
- ½ tablespoon cider or wine vinegar
- 3 to 4 tablespoons of olive, safflower, peanut, or corn oil
- Salt and pepper to taste

Needed

- Paring knife and chef's knife
- Egg slicer

- ➢ Strainer or colander
- ➢ Large platter

1) Lay the lettuce leaves nicely on an oval or round platter.

2) Peel tomatoes after plunging them a few seconds in boiling water. Slice them and arrange them on the lettuce leaves.

3) Slice the eggs with an egg slicer or cut them in quarters or halves and place on the tomatoes.

4) Drain the sardines, save the oil for the dressing, and arrange the sardines on top in a spoke fashion. If you use the tuna in oil, drain the oil and place the tuna in the center on the lettuce leaves.

5) Prepare vinaigrette by placing garlic in a small bowl. Mix well with the mustard, vinegar, and add oil. Salt and pepper to taste. Pour the dressing on the salad just before serving.

Anchovy Butter
Beurre d'anchois

Use this as a spread on toasted baguette or to fill up small vegetables like cherry tomatoes, mushroom caps. Anchovy butter can also be used on top of a steak, a piece of fish, or blanched vegetables. It gives a rare and rich flavor on either one of them. Try it!

Yield 1 cup   Easy

- A 2 ounce can of anchovy fillets in olive oil drained
- 3 to 4 cloves of garlic
- ¼ cup minced parsley, curly or flat
- 1 tablespoon red wine or cider vinegar
- 2 sticks of unsalted butter at room temperature (225 grams)
- ⅛ teaspoon black pepper
- 1 baguette toasted

Needed

- ➢ Food processor or a mortar and pestle
- ➢ Measuring cups and spoons

1) Mash the first 3 ingredients using a mortar and pestle or food processor. Add the vinegar, butter, and pepper. Process to a smooth paste.
2) Spread on toasted baguette slices for appetizers.

Tips

You can keep it in the fridge for several days in an airtight container.

Canapés

Canapés are open faced tea or cocktail sandwiches. As I was growing up my parents often had friends over for Sunday afternoon tea, coffee, or aperitif, usually around the holidays. These are great for happy hour, any kind of reception, holiday party or high tea.

My dad loved to create various sandwiches with different spreads and toppings. The prettiest type is open faced and called a canapé. This allows you to see what you are about to taste. No surprise fillings!

This has no measurements. Your imagination and what you have on hand will guide you. Be creative, experiment and find out what you and your family like.

Allow 6 to 8 canapés per person   Easy

Bread

- Thin sliced sturdy bread that does not fall apart when cut.
- Pumpernickel or rye cocktail bread work well.
- Toasting is always an option.

Utensils and canapé shapes

- Use cookie cutters to make attractive and varied shapes. You can also cut shapes with a knife.
- Tin canapé bread molds come in a variety of shapes for baking your own bread.

Spreads

- All spreads should be at room temperature. A good base is mayonnaise, as is softened butter, mustard, cream cheese, anchovy paste, liver sausage, tapenade, guacamole, pesto, or blue cheese mixed with softened butter and blended until smooth.
- Butter can be whipped with ½ teaspoon of lemon juice, Worcestershire

sauce, or 1 tablespoon of horseradish, with chives, chopped parsley or even curry powder.

- Use equal amounts of mayonnaise and mustard for a *rémoulade* flavor.
- If you want to make sweet canapés you could use cream cheese or mascarpone, topped with any kind of sliced fruit.

Toppings

- Cucumber slices, tomato slices, red radishes slices, walnut, or pecan halves, sliced hardboiled egg, shredded chicken, shrimp, smoked salmon, Swiss cheese, salami, or prosciutto.
- Prosciutto, salami, and smoked salmon can be rolled up and presented as a rose on top of the spread.

Garnishes

- Keep some sprigs of dill, chives, mint leaves, olives, pimiento strips, cornichons/pickles, rolled anchovies and capers as the garnish to put on top of your topping.
- Use your imagination and taste all the time as you perfect your spreads with the toppings.

Sardine spread

- 1 can sardines in olive oil
- 1 stick of butter at room temperature (113 grams)
- The juice of ½ lemon – about 2 tablespoons
- A few sprigs minced parsley

1) Mash everything with a fork until smooth. Spread on the bread and decorate with slices of red radishes.

Samples of a canapé tray

1) Small rounds of bread spread with butter, topped with cucumber slices
2) Small rounds of bread spread with sardine spread and topped with red radishes slices

3) Squares of bread spread with liver sausage or smooth pâté, topped with red pimiento cross and small onion circles

4) Small rounds of bread spread with mayonnaise, topped with the mashed white of a hardboiled egg, and half an olive

5) Squares of bread spread with blue cheese and butter, top with walnut halves

6) Small rounds of bread spread with mayonnaise, topped with the mashed yolk of a hardboiled egg, a slice of tomato and a slice of pickle

7) Squares of bread spread with butter, topped with a slice of Swiss cheese and a red pimiento strip

8) Small rounds of bread spread with mayonnaise, topped with a slice of hardboiled egg, topped with a rolled anchovy and ½ an olive

9) Rectangles of bread, spread with sardine spread, topped with half slices of cucumber overlapping with half slices of tomatoes

10) Hearts of bread spread with cream cheese mixed with minced lettuce, topped with a rose of smoked salmon and a dill sprig or a caper on top

These are just ideas. I could go on forever. Let your imagination and taste do the work!

Tips

Canapés can be made ahead of time and refrigerated, covered so they do not dry out. Be aware that if your spread is too wet, it will make the bread soggy. Toasting the bread beforehand often helps. You should not make them more than 2 hours ahead of time. Have an assembly line if you have several family members or friends around.

Celeriac salad
Céleri rémoulade

To me raw celery does not have any taste. I do like the flavor of cooked celery but what I like the best is celery root also called celeriac in the USA.

This is not a popular item in the USA but in France we often have a "céleri rémoulade" as an appetizer. It is unbelievably easy to make! Try it, you might like it.

Serves 4 to 6   Easy

- 1 small to medium size head of celery root (usually sold with the root vegetables) ½ to ¾ pound (227 to 340 grams)
- 2 tablespoons lemon juice (about ½ a medium lemon)
- 1 teaspoon of salt

Rémoulade Sauce

- 1 large egg yolk at room temperature
- 2 tablespoons of Dijon mustard at room temperature
- 2 tablespoons of vinegar at room temperature

- ½ to 1 cup of safflower oil at room temperature
- Salt and pepper
- 2 tablespoons of chopped parsley (optional)

Needed

- ➢ Vegetable peeler or paring knife
- ➢ Grater or the grater attachment on your food processor
- ➢ Hand mixer or food processor

1) Peel the head of celery and grate it. It should yield between 4 and 5 cups of grated celery root. Pour the juice of the lemon on it so it does not darken. Put it in a bowl with 1 teaspoon of salt and let marinate for 30 minutes to 1 hour.

2) Drain it and squeeze the juice out between your hands.

3) Make the sauce the same way you make the mayonnaise on page 10. The difference is the remoulade has more mustard and vinegar. If the mustardy flavor is too much for you use less. Mix the egg yolk with the mustard, the vinegar and salt and pepper in a food processor or with a hand mixer. As you are beating that mixture, pour a trickle of oil at a time and beat on high speed. The sauce should thicken.

4) If the sauce is too thick you can thin it with a little vinegar or warm water.

5) Mix part of the sauce with the drained and shredded celeriac. Let sit for about 30 minutes so the flavors mature. The grated celery absorbs a lot of the sauce. You can prepare it 1 to 2 hours ahead.

Tips

When you buy the head of celery, tap on it before you buy it. If it sounds full and it is heavy, that is the one to buy. If it sounds hollow, it will not be good. If you put the head of celery in boiling water for 1 minute, it will be more tender, and it will not have the sharp flavor. If you have some sauce leftover, you can refrigerate it and use it with cold chicken, cold fish, or use it in salads. If your mayonnaise/rémoulade is made with fresh eggs, it can keep in the fridge for several days.

For an easy rémoulade use 1-2 tablespoons mayonnaise, mixed with 1-2 tablespoon of Dijon mustard, and 1 tablespoon vinegar.

Greek Style Marinated Mushrooms

Champignons à la grecque

My dad used to make this for special occasions. It is quite easy and a great appetizer for cocktails. He learned it from attending a cooking class from groundbreaking cookbook author Françoise Bernard who wrote the 1963 classic "Les recettes faciles de Françoise Bernard".

Serves 4 to 6   Easy

- 1⅓ cup water
- 5 tablespoons dry white wine
- 8 tablespoons lemon juice (or the equivalent in cider vinegar)
- A small branch fennel
- 1 stick celery
- 12 grains of coriander or in powder form
- 1 bay leaf
- 1 sprig of thyme
- 2 sugar cubes or 3 teaspoons of granulated sugar (to sweeten the broth that would be too sour because of the lemon juice)
- 10 black peppercorns
- ½ teaspoon salt
- 1 pound button mushrooms
- 10 small pearl onions
- 5 tablespoons olive oil

Needed

- ➢ Medium saucepan
- ➢ Square of cheese cloth

1) If using fresh herbs and spices place them in a tied cheesecloth pouch for easy retrieval. This is not necessary if they are powdered.
2) In a saucepan bring to a boil the water, white wine, lemon juice, fennel, celery, coriander, bay leaf, thyme, sugar cubes, peppercorns, and salt. Boil for 10 minutes.
3) Clean the mushrooms, cutting part of the foot and brushing them with a wet towel. If they are too big you can cut them in quarters. Peel the onions.
4) Put the prepared mushrooms and onions in the same saucepan adding the olive oil. Cover and boil for 6 to 8 minutes.
5) Refrigerate for 2 to 3 hours. Remove the spices and the aromatic herbs before serving and pour out the liquid.
6) Serve cold as an appetizer with toothpicks.

Tips

The sugar cuts the acidity of the lemon juice. If you are allergic to citrus, you can substitute with wine or cider vinegars.

Eggs in Red Wine Sauce

Oeufs en meurette

Growing up in Burgundy this was often a first course option in every gastronomic restaurant we went to, for Sunday lunch. It was a favorite of my dad.

Serves 4   Intermediate

- 1 tablespoon of butter (14 grams)
- ⅓ cup bacon, about 1 slice diced
- 1 or 2 medium size cloves of garlic minced
- 4 medium shallots minced
- 1 cup of sliced button mushrooms (150 grams)
- 1 tablespoon of flour
- 1 ½ cups red wine
- 1 bouquet garni made from 1 bay leaf, 1 branch of thyme, 1 branch parsley tied with string to ease removal. Or use 1 teaspoon each of dried herbs.
- 4 to 8 baguette slices spread with olive oil
- 2 tablespoons of any vinegar
- 1 or 2 large eggs per person
- Salt and pepper to taste
- Chopped parsley for garnish
- Some *beurre manié*, a thickener made with 1 tablespoon of room temperature butter mashed in 1 tablespoon of flour

Needed

- ➤ Frying pan
- ➤ Large saucepan

1) Preheat oven to 400°F.

2) Put the butter in a frying pan and add the bacon, shallots, garlic, and mushrooms.

3) When everything is golden, add the flour and mix well. Pour the red wine gradually until the sauce thickens. Add the bouquet garni, salt and pepper.

4) The sauce can boil a little, then lower the heat and simmer for 20 to 25 minutes. The sauce should be smooth and coat a spoon. If it is too runny use the *beurre manié* to thicken.

5) Grill the oiled baguette slices in the oven for 3 to 4 minutes and set them aside.

6) At the last minute you can prepare the eggs and poach them in boiling water and vinegar. Make circles with a spoon in the water/vinegar. Break one egg in a small ramequin and gently slide into the boiling water. Poach for 4 to 5 minutes while using a spoon to envelop the egg with the filaments of the egg whites. Remove egg with slotted spoon and drain on a paper towel and repeat the same process for each egg.

7) Pour some red wine sauce on a soup plate, add 1 or 2 slices of crispy baguette on the sides, and place the poached egg on top of the sauce.

8) Serve immediately with sprinkled chopped parsley.

Tips

To simplify the poaching process, you can also use egg poaching cups, some of which float on the water, and you can break one egg in each cup. You can poach them for 5 minutes. A lot easier!

Another way of preparing those eggs is to put the sauce in a buttered ramequin and breaking one egg over it. Top the egg with a little sauce and bake in a 400°F oven for 10 to 12 minutes.

This could be served for brunch or a light supper too.

Pâte à choux

Pâte à choux —pronounced "paaht ah shoo" is a twice cooked dough, once on the stove and secondly in the oven. It can be used to create an infinite variety of sweet and savory treats. With familiarity, the dough is made quickly from the same ratio of ingredients: 1 cup of water + 1 stick of butter, 1 cup of flour and 4 large eggs.

Choux pastry is very versatile. You can make gougères – which are cheese puffs, cocktail savory appetizers filled with a cold or hot filling – quenelles -- a poached fish or chicken choux dough from Lyon, served with a sauce, beignets of potatoes, called Pommes Dauphine in French, éclairs, religieuses, another choux dessert with chocolate or coffee pastry cream, profiteroles often dipped in chocolate or beautiful swans. Other variations to explore include croquembouches, Paris-Brest-- a circular cake filled with hazelnut cream, made in honor of the bicycle race between Paris and Brest, Saint-Honoré--a choux pastry circular cake filled with whipped cream, to honor the patron of bakers and chouquettes -- little choux with pearl sugar on top.

There are several secrets:

- Choux pastry is at its best, fresh. So, plan accordingly. In most cases, you may want to have your filling done in advance.
- Make sure you dry the dough a few minutes by putting it back on the stove, after you have mixed the flour with the water/butter mixture off the heat.
- Leave the door of the oven ajar after you have cooked the choux and turned off the heat, so they dry a bit (2-3 minutes).
- A good baker knows his/her oven well. Check your oven temperature with an oven thermometer. Use it as your guide to the correct baking temperature.

Cocktail Savory Little Choux

Petits choux apéro

Makes 20 little cocktail choux   Intermediate

- 1 cup of water (240 grams)
- 1 stick of butter (113 grams)
- A pinch of salt
- 1 cup of flour (120 grams)
- 4 large eggs

Needed

- Medium saucepan
- Baking sheet
- Stand mixer or handheld mixer (optional)
- A tablespoon
- Piping bag with ½" tip (optional)

1) Preheat the oven to 425°F.

2) On stove bring to a boil the water, butter, and salt.

3) Remove from heat and add the flour all at once. Mix vigorously with a wooden spoon until all the flour is absorbed.

4) Return dough to the heat and stir to dry 2 to 3 minutes. The dough is dry when it comes cleanly off the sides forming a film on the bottom of the pan and can be shaped into a smooth ball.

5) Remove from heat and add dough to stand mixer or hand mixing bowl. Stir to release steam and heat and add one egg at a time, mixing well after each addition. The dough should be smooth and a pipeable consistency.

6) Refrigerate for 30 minutes to improve oven rise.

7) On a greased cookie sheet place 12 to 20 equal amounts of dough using a pastry bag with ½" tip or tablespoon.

8) Bake the 12 medium choux for about 20 to 25 minutes. If baking 20 small choux reduce time to 10 to 15 minutes. Pastry is done when it is a deep golden brown.

9) When done, turn oven off, crack door open and allow pastry to slowly dry out and cool for 15 minutes before removing from the oven. This is a critical step that allows pastry to dry, firm up, and insure against collapse.

10) When out of the oven and cooled, they can be immediately filled by either injection with a piping bag or by cutting in half and filling with spoon.

Filling ideas

Warm—Ham and grated Gruyère cheese, chicken with a mornay sauce, chicken with a hunter sauce, crab with a mornay sauce or any other sauce with fish or meat. Be creative!!

Cold—Tuna salad, cold chicken with mayonnaise sauce, mixed vegetables with mayonnaise sauce, guacamole and shrimp, smoked salmon with goat cheese, prosciutto, mascarpone and olives, tomatoes, mozzarella and basil. Again, be creative!!!

Gougères

These are little cheese cream puffs that can be served as a snack or an appetizer. They are a specialty from Burgundy where I grew up and are often served with an aperitif, like kir, a classic in Burgundy.

Wine cellars are called caves in Burgundy, and these are often served there. They date to the 13th century.

Yield 12 to 14 medium or 20 small   Intermediate

- 1 cup water
- 1 stick of butter (113 grams)
- 1 cup of flour (120 grams)
- A pinch of salt
- 4 large eggs
- ¾ to 1 cup of shredded Gruyère cheese (110 grams)

Needed

- ➢ Medium saucepan
- ➢ Measuring cups and spoons

- A wooden spoon
- Stand or handheld mixer
- Cookie Sheet

1) Preheat the oven to 425°F.
2) On stove bring to a boil the water, butter, and salt.
3) Remove from heat and add the flour all at once. Mix vigorously with a wooden spoon until all the flour is absorbed.
4) Return dough to the heat and stir to dry 2 to 3 minutes. The dough is dry when it comes cleanly off the sides forming a film on the bottom of the pan and can be shaped into a smooth ball.
5) Remove from heat and add dough to stand mixer or hand mixing bowl. Stir to release steam and heat and add one egg at a time, mixing well after each addition. Add the cheese to mixture. The dough should be smooth.
6) Refrigerate for 30 minutes to improve oven rise.
7) Drop tablespoons of dough on a greased cookie sheet.
8) Bake the 12 medium choux for about 20 to 25 minutes. If baking 20 small choux reduce time to 10 to 15 minutes. Pastry is done when it is a deep golden brown.
9) When done, turn oven off, crack door open and allow pastry to slowly dry out and cool for 15 minutes before removing from the oven. This is a critical step that allows pastry to dry, firm up, and insure against collapse.

Potato Salad with Chunky Tuna

Pommes de terre en salade aux miettes de thon

This was a favorite appetizer or first course for lunch at my parents' house in spring and summer. My mom liked to use chunky tuna in oil, so it gives some extra flavor to the potatoes that are otherwise bland in a salad.

Serves 4 to 6   Easy

- 1 ½ pound new potatoes, red or Yukon Gold (about 750 grams)
- 1 can of chunky tuna in oil
- 1 handful of chopped parsley or chives for garnish

Vinaigrette

- 1 to 2 cloves garlic minced
- ½ tablespoon Dijon mustard
- ½ tablespoon cider or wine vinegar
- 3 to 4 tablespoons of olive, safflower, peanut, or corn oil
- Salt and pepper to taste

Needed

- A saucepan
- A paring knife
- A medium size glass bowl
- A small mixing bowl
- Salad tongs

1) Boil unpeeled potatoes for 25 to 30 minutes.

2) Peel them while still warm and cube.

3) Make the vinaigrette, mixing all the ingredients in the order given, in small mixing bowl

4) Pour the vinaigrette and the chunky tuna, with the oil on top of the potatoes and mix well.

5) Top with chopped parsley or chives.

Tips

This salad is delicious when made with small new potatoes.

If you can serve this salad lukewarm or warm, the potatoes taste better. As much as possible, try to prepare this salad at the last minute. You can add gherkins, cornichons, small pickles or one chopped hardboiled egg.

Red Beets Salad
Salade de betteraves rouges

This was another favorite at my parent's house as an appetizer for lunch, especially in the summer. In France, you can buy these already cooked at any supermarket or even in the outdoor markets. Some stores carry them precooked.

Serves 4 persons					Easy

- 1 large or 2 medium red beets cooked and peeled (300 to 400 grams)

Vinaigrette

- 1 to 2 cloves garlic minced
- ½ tablespoon Dijon mustard
- ½ tablespoon cider or wine vinegar
- 3 to 4 tablespoons of olive, safflower, peanut, or corn oil
- Salt and pepper to taste

Needed

- Paring knife
- Small glass bowl
- Small mixing bowl
- Salad tongs

1) Cook whole beets in simmering water for 30 minutes, or quarter to shorten cooking time. Pierce with a knife, they will be tender when ready. Cool before peeling.

2) Peel with a paring knife and cut in thin slices or ½ inch cubes. Place in a glass bowl.

3) Place garlic in a small bowl. Mix well with the mustard, vinegar, and add oil. Salt and pepper to taste. Pour the dressing on the beets. They can marinate for an hour before serving.

Grated Carrot Salad

Salade de carottes râpées

This salad was another standard at my parents' house and often served as crudités in restaurants and bistros with beet, potato, or cucumber salad, all on one plate.

Serves 4 to 6   Easy

- ½ pound grated or 10 ounces bag of shredded carrots (284 grams)
- 1 tablespoon of lemon juice

Vinaigrette

- 1 to 2 cloves garlic minced
- ½ tablespoon Dijon mustard
- ½ tablespoon cider or wine vinegar
- 3 to 4 tablespoons of olive, safflower, peanut, or corn oil
- Salt and pepper to taste

Needed

- Grater or grating attachment food processor
- Glass bowl
- Small mixing bowl
- Salad tongs

1) Grate the carrots in a bowl and cover with lemon juice to preserve color.
2) Make the vinaigrette in a mixing bowl in the order given and pour over the carrots.

Tips

You can replace the vinegar in the dressing with lemon juice for a different flavor.

Grated carrots are much more pleasant to eat than shredded carrots. Try to grate them rather than eat the store-bought shredded ones which are too crunchy.

It can mature in the fridge for a few days which improves flavor.

Tomato Salad
Salade de tomates

My parents served this at our house for a first course, especially in the summer. The summer tomatoes are so meaty and flavorful! At our house it was always made with peeled tomatoes. The difference is worth the time. With peeled tomatoes, the salad melts in your mouth!

Serves 4 to 6   Easy

- 1 pound tomatoes (450 grams)
- 1 tablespoon of chopped parsley for garnish

Vinaigrette

- 1 to 2 cloves garlic minced
- ½ tablespoon Dijon mustard
- ½ tablespoon cider or wine vinegar
- 3 to 4 tablespoons of olive, safflower, peanut, or corn oil
- Salt and pepper to taste

Needed

- Saucepan
- Paring knife
- Round, square, or a rectangular serving dish
- Salad tongs

1) Cut a shallow cross through the skin of the tomato on the blossom end.

2) Submerge one tomato at a time in boiling water for 5 seconds. Remove from the water and peel off skin starting from the blossom end. Repeat in this manner for all the tomatoes.

3) Slice the tomatoes and arrange in overlapping pattern on a serving dish.

4) Combine vinaigrette in the order given, mix well and pour over tomatoes.

5) Sprinkle with chopped parsley.

Tips

In winter and spring, tomatoes have a lot of liquid. After they are sliced, it is a good idea to sprinkle some salt over them and let them marinate for 30 minutes. Afterwards, drain them and proceed as above.

Niçoise Salad

Salade Niçoise

This is a specialty from Nice on the French Riviera, but you can eat this salad all throughout the southeast of France. Traditionally, there are no potatoes, but my family and I have always used some.

You can serve it as a main dish for lunch or for dinner in the summer.

Serves 6 to 8   Easy

- 1 head of butter lettuce
- 2 medium Yukon Gold boiled potatoes cut in 1-inch cubes
- ½ pound blanched French green beans (227 grams)
- 1 well drained 7 ounce can of tuna, preferably oil packed (200 grams)
- ½ English cucumber thinly sliced
- 2 medium peeled tomatoes cut in wedges
- 2 large hard-boiled eggs quartered
- 1 average size green, yellow, orange, or red pepper cut in strips
- 1 medium red, sweet, or white onion sliced thin
- 1 can of flat anchovy fillets
- 10 black olives, Greek or Niçoise

Vinaigrette

- 1 to 2 cloves garlic or 1 shallot minced
- ½ tablespoon Dijon mustard
- ½ tablespoon cider or wine vinegar

- 3 to 4 tablespoons of olive, safflower, peanut, or corn oil
- Salt and pepper to taste

Needed

- Paring knife
- Large serving platter
- Salad tongs
- Small mixing bowl

To assemble salad

1) Line a platter with lettuce leaves. Dome cubed potatoes in middle.
2) Blanch the green beans by plunging them in boiling water for 5 minutes and then immediately in ice water. Arrange the green beans around the potatoes, and the tuna on top of the potatoes.
3) Place the sliced cucumber around on top of the beans.
4) Put the tomato wedges alternating with the quartered eggs all around the dish.
5) Place strips of peppers and sliced onions here and there.
6) Place the anchovy fillets in a spoke fashion or in a lattice fashion on top of the potatoes and tuna.
7) Place the olives in between the anchovy fillets. Pour the vinaigrette over, just before serving.

For vinaigrette

1) Mix that dressing in a bowl in the order given.
2) Pour over the salad at the last minute since the dressing might burn the greens if left too long on the lettuce, or each person can add his/her own dressing.

Tips

You can use rolled anchovies with a caper in the middle instead of flat anchovy fillets. The eggs may be sliced instead of quartered. Be creative!

Cucumber Salad
Salade de concombre

My mom, Mamie Gisèle, would make this appetizer salad for lunch, with her trademark vinaigrette, at least once a week, in the late spring and summer. She would love to use garlic in her salad dressing. On the other hand, my aunt Jeanne loved to use minced shallot. So, see what you like, and experiment! This is usually served as a first course.

Serves 4 to 6   Easy

- 1 English cucumber (about 400 grams)
- 1 teaspoon salt

Vinaigrette

- 1 to 2 cloves garlic or shallot minced
- ½ tablespoon Dijon mustard
- ½ tablespoon cider or wine vinegar
- 3 to 4 tablespoons of olive, safflower, peanut, or corn oil
- Salt and pepper to taste

Needed

- Vegetable peeler
- Paring knife
- Medium glass bowl
- Small mixing bowl
- Salad tongs

1) Peel and deseed cucumber by cutting in half and scraping out the seeds with a spoon. Slice very thin. Place it in a medium glass bowl and cover with the salt. Let it sit for 1 hour, so the salt releases the juices. Then squeeze the slices tightly to extract as much liquid as possible.

2) Prepare the vinaigrette and pour over the cucumber slices. Check the seasoning again.

Tips

For a creamier salad dressing, you can mix 1 tablespoon of sour cream with 1 tablespoon of mayonnaise.

Green Salad

Salade verte

In France we eat green salad, usually the equivalent of a Boston lettuce, after the main course to refresh our palate before the cheese and dessert courses. Of course, you can use mesclun, arugula or a combination of greens with radicchio.

Forget those expensive store-bought dressings that are loaded with sugar and calories. You can make your own at a fraction of the cost.

This salad dressing, I have watched my mom make it every day for most green salads and other vegetable salads like shredded carrot salad, red beets salad, tomato salad, potato salad, cucumber salad.

The quantity of vinegar and oil is 1 volume of vinegar for 3-4 of oil. You can put as much mustard as you want. See what you like and be creative.

Serves as desired   Easy

Vinaigrette

- 1 to 2 cloves garlic minced or 1 minced shallot
- ½ tablespoon Dijon mustard
- ½ tablespoon cider or wine vinegar
- 3 to 4 tablespoons of olive, safflower, peanut, or corn oil
- Salt and pepper to taste

Needed

- Spoon
- A garlic press
- A small bowl
- Measuring cups and spoons

- ➢ A salad bowl
- ➢ Salad tongs

1) Figure about 2 or 3 leaves of lettuce per person.

2) Mix that dressing in a bowl in the order given. Pour as desired over the salad and mix with salad tongs at the last minute since the dressing might burn the greens if left too long on the lettuce. You can add a chopped hard-boiled egg, parmesan, feta, or anchovy for a different flavor.

Tips

If you want to make dressing in a bottle for a week, you can triple or quadruple the proportions and keep it on the kitchen counter if it does not contain garlic. If you refrigerate you may need to bring to room temperature to serve.

Cheese Soufflé

Soufflé au fromage

My dad was fascinated by soufflés and some Sundays, it would be his mission to make either a cheese soufflé or a Grand Marnier soufflé.

A lot of cooks are intimidated by soufflés, but they are quite simple to make. They just cannot be done ahead of time. Soufflé success depends on good advance preparation of all the ingredients so it can come directly out of the oven to the table at the last minute.

My mom always said: "Le soufflé n'attend pas mais ce sont les convives qui attendent le soufflé!" "The soufflé waits for no one; it is the guests who wait for the soufflé!"

Serves 4 to 6   Intermediate

For a 4 cup soufflé dish

- 1 tablespoon softened butter and 1 tablespoon all-purpose flour for the mold
- 3 tablespoons unsalted butter (43 grams)
- 3 tablespoons all-purpose flour (23 grams)
- 1 cup of whole milk

- Salt and pepper
- 3 large eggs at room temperature and separated
- 1 cup shredded Gruyère or Comté cheese (110grams)
- Grated nutmeg
- A pinch of salt in the egg whites

Needed

- 4 cup ovenproof soufflé dish or four 8 to 10-ounce ovenproof soufflé ramequins
- Saucepan
- Whisk
- Clean and dry mixing bowl
- Spatula

1) Preheat oven to 400°F with cookie sheet on middle rack.

2) Butter a 4-cup soufflé dish or individual dishes sprinkling with flour to dust the interior. Put in the fridge. If you are planning to fill the dish to the rim, butter and flour a parchment paper collar and tie it with a string around the top of the dish so the soufflé can rise.

3) Make a roux, melting the butter on medium heat in a saucepan for a few minutes. When the butter is sizzling, add the flour, and stir well. When the mixture is foaming, add the cold milk gradually and stir continuously without stopping on medium high heat with a whisk. You now have a thick béchamel sauce.

4) Off the heat, add one egg yolk at a time and stir well. When they are all incorporated, add all the grated cheese. Taste and add salt and pepper and grated nutmeg according to your taste.

5) In a separate clean and dry bowl, beat the egg whites with a pinch of salt until they look like snow with peaks but not too firm. Fold gently half of the whites to the cheese mixture, with a spatula trying to incorporate a maximum of air. Fold the second half of the whites.

6) Pour into the prepared dish or dishes. It should be ⅔ to ¾ full. If not, then use the paper collar above mentioned. The soufflé is all about air!

7) Place the dish on top of the hot cookie sheet.

8) If you have a single soufflé dish, bake for 25 to 28 minutes. If you have individual small ramequins, it should take about 15 to 20 minutes.

Tips

The salt in the egg whites will help them to be beaten stiffer.

Placing the soufflé dish in the fridge helps it rise higher. As does the preheated cookie sheet.

Put the soufflé in the oven 30 minutes before you plan to eat it.

Do not open the oven door! No peaking or the soufflé will not rise!

Country Pâté

Terrine

My aunt Jeanne who lived in the countryside in the Limousin region of France used to raise rabbits, chicken, and her neighbors would raise pigs. So, she would often make all kinds of pâtés grinding the meat with a grinder she would crank by hand. My dad, her younger brother, learned from her and of course, he would make liver, pork, and rabbit pâté. This is a recipe I have reconstituted from memory.

Serves 10 as an appetizer or 6 as a main course   Easy

- 1 pound ground pork (450 to 500 grams)
- 2 large eggs
- 4 ounces ground pork liver, ½ cup (100 to 110 grams)
- ¼ cup minced red, yellow, or white onion (52 grams)
- 8 tablespoons chopped parsley (12 grams)
- 1½ tablespoons minced garlic (24grams)
- 1½ teaspoons kosher salt (27 grams)
- 1 teaspoon freshly ground pepper (3 grams)

- ½ teaspoon or more of Four Spices-Quatre Epices (see recipe below)

Recipe of Four Spices:

- 1 teaspoon ground cloves/ 1 teaspoon ground nutmeg/ 2 teaspoons ground cinnamon/ 1 tablespoon white pepper (if you want you can add 1 teaspoon of ground coriander). You can vary the quantity of each spice according to your taste.

Needed

- ➤ Meat grinder if meat is not already ground
- ➤ Food processor or a chef knife
- ➤ Large bowl
- ➤ Ovenproof earthenware dish
- ➤ Aluminum foil

1) Preheat the oven to 350°F.
2) Grease a 1½ quart size crock or earthenware terrine with either butter or oil.
3) Mix all the ingredients with the spices in a bowl then put everything in the terrine. Pack it tight and put a lid on it or cover with aluminum foil. Make a little hole for the steam to escape. Most terrine dishes have a little hole. If you want a crust on the top of the pâté remove the cover.
4) Place the terrine in the middle of the oven until the inside of the pâté reaches 160°F, after about 1 hour and 20 minutes.
5) Remove from the oven and let cool at room temperature for several hours.

Tips

You can add things like olives or pistachios, so when the pâté is cut it is decorated on the inside. On the top you can put bay leaves or a bacon slice for flavor.

It is better to let it cool before cutting. It will cut easier and not fall apart.

You can keep the pâté for at least a week. You could freeze it too!

Serve as an appetizer with crackers, sliced baguette, as a main course with a salad and pickles, grainy mustard, for a picnic, an easy lunch or dinner during the week or on the weekend.

Soups

Provençal Fish Stew 66

French Onion Soup 70

Chanterelles Chowder 72

Winter Vegetable Soup 74

Provençal Fish Stew

Bouillabaisse

When my parents took us to the French Riviera for summer vacations, I kept a great memory of the first bouillabaisse I had in a restaurant located between La Ciotat and Hyères near the National Park of the Calanques.

When we went to Sainte Maries de la Mer with my husband Jean, many years later, we had a scrumptious bouillabaisse. When I returned to the USA, I had to recreate this meal for my family. It has now become a tradition at Christmas time.

Bouillabaisse in the Occitan language is "bolhabaissa" a compound word that consists of two verbs; "bolhir" which means to boil and "abaissar" which means to lower the heat. You will see that technique used in the boiling of the broth followed by a lower simmer for the soft fish, crustaceans, and shellfish.

You can make this recipe even quicker and easier by skipping the sautéing of the vegetables at the beginning. Put the first 12 ingredients in the enamel cast iron Dutch oven and boil for 30 minutes. Then proceed to add the cut-up fish.

Serves 6 to 8   Easy

For Bouillabaisse

- ½ cup olive oil

- 2 large garlic cloves minced
- 1 box of Mirepoix, about 15 ounces, or 1 large onion diced, 3 medium size carrots diced, and 2 medium size celery branches diced
- ¼ cup chopped parsley
- 1 bouquet garni made from 1 bay leaf, 1 branch of thyme, 1 branch parsley tied with string to ease removal. Or use 1 teaspoon each of dried herbs.
- 1 pinch dry or fresh chopped basil
- 1 28 ounce can of peeled and chopped tomatoes
- 1 teaspoon saffron or 1 tablespoon paprika
- Salt and pepper to taste
- 1 large piece dried orange peel
- 1 cup white wine
- 2 cups water, fish stock, clam juice or even chicken stock
- 6 toasted baguette slices brushed with olive oil, toasted, and then rubbed with garlic
- Firm fish like halibut, wild salmon, monkfish, cod, or sturgeon
- Soft fish like farm raised salmon, sole, sea bass, or whiting
- Crustaceans and shellfish like shrimp, crab, lobster tails, scallops, mussels, clams
- Use a combination and variety of seafood, for example:

    2 steaks of halibut, wild salmon, cod, or sea bass (450 grams)

    ½ pound shredded crabmeat (225 grams)

    ½ pound big shrimp, king prawns or jumbo shrimp (225 grams)

    ½ pound scallops, mussels, or clams (225 grams)

For rouille/red pepper sauce

- ¼ cup roasted red peppers either in a jar or roasted at home and puréed (22 grams)

- 4 large garlic cloves
- 1 large egg yolk
- ¼ cup white bread dipped in the broth and squeezed out
- 1 teaspoon of thyme
- 4 to 6 tablespoons extra virgin olive oil
- Salt and pepper to taste

Needed

- ➢ Large 5 to 6-quart enamel cast iron Dutch oven like a Le Creuset or Staub
- ➢ Food processor

Bouillabaisse

1) Preheat oven to 400°F.
2) Place the oil in an enamel cast iron pot on medium heat. When hot, add the prepared onion, carrots, celery and cook until translucent.
3) Add the garlic, and sauté for a few more minutes.
4) Add the herbs, then the tomatoes, saffron, the orange peel, the white wine, and the broth. Cook on medium high heat covered for 20 to 30 minutes. During that time, cut the fish in large cubes.
5) Add the cubed firm fish first then cook uncovered on medium heat for 10 minutes.
6) Turn the heat to medium low. Add the cubed soft fish, the crustaceans and shellfish and cook for 5 minutes covered.
7) Prepare the slices of baguettes by brushing both sides with olive oil. Place in oven for 3 to 4 minutes. Once they are golden, rub them with a clove of garlic.
8) The broth can be eaten separately from the fish in the French style or combined with the seafood San Francisco style.
9) Serve with the garlic toasts.

Rouille/red pepper sauce

Use when serving the fish separately French style

1) Place all the ingredients in a food processor except for the olive oil.

2) Using the opening on the top of the food processor, pour the olive oil in a trickle.

3) The sauce should thicken and become like a mayonnaise. Adjust the seasoning.

Tips

You can add some Tabasco, Piment d'Espelette, paprika or saffron if you want.

French Onion Soup

Gratinée lyonnaise

My dad loved to make onion soup. He would talk constantly about the onion soups he had in the Lyon traditional restaurants called "bouchons" during his business trips. He would often ask to make it at home for Sunday dinner. As a child it was never a favorite of mine because of the bread in the soup. Now I am getting older, I have a desire to make this in the winter, but I serve it with toasted baguette slices.

Serves 4 to 6   Easy

- 1 tablespoon unsalted butter (14 grams)
- 2 tablespoons safflower oil
- 3 jumbo onions sliced about 1 pound (450 grams)
- 1 or 2 cloves of garlic
- ½ cup of white wine
- 4 or 5 cups of beef or chicken stock
- 2 bay leaves
- 2 cups of shredded Gruyère cheese (226 grams)

- Salt and pepper
- 1 baguette cut in 4 or 8 slices
- Some olive oil to brush the baguette slices

Needed

- 4-6-quart enamel cast iron pot like le Creuset or Staub
- Immersion blender, food mill, or food processor
- Cookie sheet
- 4 ovenproof soup bowls

1) Preheat the oven to 400°F.
2) In an enamel cast iron pot, cook the butter and oil on medium heat. Add the onions and garlic and cook for 10 to 15 minutes.
3) Add salt and pepper. Let brown for about 10 more minutes.
4) Gradually pour the white wine and the stock, add 2 bay leaves, and let simmer for 20 minutes without the lid.
5) Remove the bay leaves. Using an immersion blender, mix the soup then taste to make sure there is enough salt and pepper.
6) Brush the baguette slices with olive oil on both sides, place on cookie sheet then brown for 3 to 4 minutes.
7) Remove baguette slices and increase oven temperature to 425°F.
8) Place 4 ovenproof soup bowls on a cookie sheet. Pour about 1 to 1 ½ cups of soup in each bowl. Place 1 or 2 slices of baguette on each bowl.
9) Sprinkle ½ cup of shredded Gruyère on each bowl. The cheese must cover all the baguette slices and the rest of the bowl.
10) Bake for 20 to 25 minutes or until the cheese is melted and browned.

Chanterelles Chowder

Soupe de girolles ou chanterelles

This is not a French recipe per se. This is a recipe from Consuelo Casey, our daughter's godmother in the USA. She was an avid mushroom hunter, and she produced this chowder recipe. We went many days in the Oregon and Washington forests to hunt for chanterelles until it became a commercial thing.

Since my family was hunting for chanterelles or "girolles" in the Limousin region of France, I thought this was appropriate to add this recipe to my book.

In France, we usually cook these chanterelles in an omelet or often with a chicken dish with a mushroom sauce. This soup is amazing, especially the next day.

Serves 4 to 6   Easy

- 1 12 ounce roll pork sausage or fresh ground pork (340 grams)
- 1 medium onion, chopped
- 2 large potatoes, diced or cubed
- 1 ⅓ pounds chopped wild mushrooms like Chanterelles or Morels (600 grams)
- 2 to 3 cups chicken broth

- Salt and pepper to taste
- A few sprigs of fresh thyme or a teaspoon of dried thyme
- 1 cup instant potato flakes
- 1 12 ounce can evaporated milk or 1 cup whipping cream
- Chopped green onions or chives for garnish
- 2 tablespoons of Worcestershire sauce (optional)

Needed

- Large soup pot
- Measuring cups and spoons

1) In a large soup pot, sauté the sausage on medium heat until lightly brown.
2) Add the chopped onions and cook until translucent. Add the potatoes, stir, and cook for 5 minutes.
3) Add the chopped mushrooms and cook for 5 minutes. Add 2 cups of the broth then add salt and pepper to taste. Add the thyme sprigs. Bring to a boil.
4) Cover and simmer for 30 minutes on low heat.
5) Add the potato flakes. Stir well and cook until slightly thickened. Thin, if necessary, with reserved broth. Bring to a simmer.
6) Add the milk or cream then adjust the seasoning. Add the Worcestershire sauce if you want. Keep warm on low heat. Do not let boil.
7) Cover and let stand 15 minutes before serving.

Tips

The chowder is best made early in the day or the day before so seasonings can mature. In that case put the cream or milk in at the last minute and heat through on low heat.

Serve with chopped green onions or chives.

Winter Vegetable Soup

Soupe de légumes

This soup was a favorite in the winter at my parents' house. It can be made with water as Mamie Gisèle used to make it, but it is even more flavorful if made with chicken or other stock, homemade or purchased. If you do not have time, you can purchase broth with a low sodium content since purchased stocks have a lot of sodium.

Soups in France are not chunky like most American soups. They are more like a potage (soup puréed in a blender).

Mamie Gisèle was famous for her mixed vegetable soup. She would use more tomatoes to make it redder, more carrots to make it more orange, more watercress, leeks, or spinach to make it greener.

To serve it, she would top it with a dollop of crème fraiche and celery salt. It would be the first course of our dinner, followed by an omelet, a salad, a yogurt, or a platter of various cheeses. That would be a light dinner since lunch was the biggest meal of the day.

A note on the different terms used for soup:

Consommé: broth type -- like a beef or chicken consommé

Potage: light vegetable soup -- like a potage St Germain or potage Dubarry

Velouté or Crème: Creamy consistency -- like a crème d'asperges or velouté de champi-

gnons, usually with added cream

Bisque: usually thickened with flour and cream added -- like a shrimp or crab bisque

Soupe: general term for thick soups or chunky soups --like a soupe au pistou or soupe à l'oignon.

Serves about 8   Easy

Stock

It can be made with raw or cooked bones like beef, chicken, or vegetable scraps. You can brown the bones if raw for a deeper flavor. You do not have to add salt and pepper since you will add it when cooking your soup or sauce. You can use this stock for making soups or making sauces.

- 2 ½ to 3 quarts water
- Bones and scraps from 1 whole chicken
- 1 bay leaf
- ½ teaspoon thyme
- 1 medium onion quartered
- 5 whole peppercorns
- 2 to 3 sprigs of parsley

Needed

- 1 large stock pot with a lid
- Colander
- Large bowl
- Skimmer or large spoon

1) Bring to a boil and simmer covered for 1 hour. Cool then strain the broth. You can skim the fat or wait until it is cold and remove the top layer of fat. If you want a more concentrated stock, you can simmer it uncovered, it will reduce and have a stronger flavor.

Soup

- 2 medium red or Yukon Gold potatoes peeled and quartered
- 2 medium rutabagas peeled and quartered
- 4 medium carrots peeled and sliced
- 2 quartered tomatoes
- 1 or 2 celery stalks chopped up in 1-inch slices
- Salt and pepper
- 2 to 3 quarts chicken stock
- Crème fraiche, parsley, celery salt for serving
- Sour cream can be substituted for crème fraiche

Needed

- Large stock/soup pot
- Immersion blender, food mill, or food processor
- Ladle

1) Place the vegetables and the broth in a large pot. Bring to a boil and reduce to simmer. Cook for 30 to 40 minutes depending how big the vegetables are. The vegetables should be soft when pierced with a knife.

2) If you do not have an immersion blender, take the vegetables out, put them in a food mill, or a food processor and whirl some vegetables gradually with a little broth to help the process. When all the vegetables are blended and form a smooth purée, return to the pan, and add broth gradually until you reach the consistency you like.

3) If you have an immersion blender, you may complete the entire process in the pan. But make sure to remove some broth first and pour it in a bowl to save for later. After you blend the vegetables and part of the broth, return to heat and simmer a while as you are adding salt and pepper to your taste. If the soup is too thick for your taste you can add the broth you saved in a bowl at this point.

4) Serve in bowls with a dollop of cream, minced parsley, and celery salt.

Tips

If there is extra broth, you can add it to the left-over soup. This will make a light broth in which you can add vermicelli, alphabet noodles, tapioca, and star noodles. You will have another soup for another cold and grey day!

When my dad ate this soup, he would dilute the final remnants with red wine and drink it directly from the soup plate, an Occitan/Limousin tradition called *faire chabrot* or *chabrol*. It was a great flavor that even us kids got to try many times!

Quick Meals

Quick Meals with Crepes, Omelets and Quiches 80

Ideas for Stuffed Croissants 82

Galettes and Crepes 85

Buckwheat Crepes 87

Crepes With Cheese Sauce 89

Ham and Cheese Crepes 90

Ratatouille Crepes 90

Quick Meals with Crepes, Omelets, and Quiches

If you have flour, eggs, butter, milk, leftover vegetables, and cooked meat, you can make any of the following very quickly. Here are ideas to encourage you to be creative and experiment. Unlike baking, measurements here are more forgiving. Specific recipes can be found elsewhere in the book.

Crepes

- Make the crepes one at a time. As the crepe is cooking on the first side watch for the bubbles in the center and the brown edges on the sides. It is time to turn your crepe over and cook for 1 minute. Crepes will keep for a week in the fridge in an airtight container. You can also freeze them. They are great to have on hand for quick meals.

- When reheating a crepe, add chopped ham or cooked crumbled bacon and sprinkle with grated Gruyère Cheese. Fold the crepe in half or in quarters to allow the cheese to melt. Transfer to a plate. It is ready to eat.

- The same can be done with caramelized onions, sautéed sliced mushrooms, sliced cooked sausage and cheese.

Omelets

- You can sauté some mushrooms, or/and some onions ahead of time in some butter and oil. Mix 3 to 4 large eggs in a bowl, add salt and pepper. Pour it in a hot sizzling pan over the sautéed vegetables and you have a quick meal. You can use spinach, tomatoes. Just experiment!

- You can also mix 3 to 4 large eggs and add chives, chervil and you have an herb omelet.

- You can beat 3 to 4 large eggs in a bowl, add salt and pepper. Pour the beaten eggs in a hot nonstick pan and as it is cooking, add a handful of shredded cheese and you can eat that with a green salad.

Quiches

- You can use a store-bought pastry crust if you are pressed for time. Place the dough in a buttered pie dish, about 9 inches in diameter. You can put a handful of cut up cooked chicken, or cut up cooked sausage, spinach, broccoli, sautéed onions, or mushrooms on top of the dough.

- The base of any quiche is 3 or 4 large eggs beaten and about ¾ cup sour cream, whipping cream or even Greek yogurt. Mix well. Add salt and pepper. Pour over the meat/vegetables and add 1 cup of shredded cheese on top. Bake at 400°F for 45 minutes or until the top is golden.

- In case you do not have a pie crust, do not despair you can make the quiche with just eggs! Just be sure to butter the pan first and increase the number of large eggs to 8 and mix well with the same quantity of cream as above, vegetables and meat you want to use. Mix the cup of shredded cheese with the egg mixture. You can bake at 375°F for about 30 to 45 minutes in a medium to large muffin pan so you end up with individual portions you can freeze later for some quick lunches.

Do not be afraid to create new easy dishes for your family!

Bonne cuisine!

Ideas for Stuffed Croissants

Croissants are a buttery, flaky roll that you dip in your café or café au lait, as is, in the morning. You can also split it in half, butter it and spread jam in it. Every café on the streets of France serves these from 7:00 a.m. to 10:00 a.m.. Boulangeries have those available almost all day from 7:30 a.m. until midafternoon depending on the demand. They are best eaten fresh but whether they are fresh or a day old, here are a few ideas for fixing a quick meal.

- *French style, cut them in half and spread jam and butter.*
- *Jewish style, cut them in half and spread softened cream cheese, then top with lox or smoked salmon.*
- *Franco American style, cut them in half. Place a slice of ham and a slice of Swiss cheese on top of the ham. Put the other half of the croissant on top and place on a greased cookie sheet in a 325°F oven for 10 to 15 minutes or long enough to melt the cheese. Eat as is or with the mushroom sauce, see below.*
- *Franco Italian style, cut them in half, stuff them with sauteed mushrooms and onions and top with a mornay sauce – see sauce below but instead of mushrooms, you add ½ cup (125 grams) of shredded cheese at the end. Top the croissant with the hot mornay sauce.*
- *Anglo Saxon style, kind of like a Bostock, popular in Anglo-Saxon countries and becoming popular in France now for breakfast or for an afternoon snack. Cut the croissant in half and brush generously with a syrup, place a frangipane mixture and follow instructions below.*

Mushroom sauce for 4 croissants

- 2 tablespoons butter (28 grams)
- 2 tablespoons flour (16 grams)
- ¾ cup milk
- Salt and pepper
- Grated nutmeg
- ¼ pound sliced and sauteed mushrooms (112 grams)

Needed

- Small saucepan
- Whisk

1) Melt the butter in a saucepan. When sizzling, add all the flour and with a whisk, stir and cook till foaming. Add the cold milk gradually whisking constantly until it thickens. Add salt and pepper to taste and some grated nutmeg.
2) Add the mushrooms and pour the heated sauce over the croissants. You have a quick hot lunch.

Frangipane for 4 croissants

- ½ cup almond flour (56 grams)
- ¼ cup granulated sugar (50 grams)
- 1 large egg
- ¼ cup softened unsalted butter (57 grams)
- ½ teaspoon almond extract
- 3 to 4 tablespoons sliced almonds
- Powdered sugar to sprinkle

Hot syrup for 4 croissants

- ½ cup water
- ¼ cup granulated sugar (50 grams)
- 1 tablespoon flavoring like rum or kirsch

Needed

- Stand or handheld mixer
- Cookie sheet
- Small saucepan

1) Mix all ingredients with a mixer. Beat until light and fluffy. Your frangipane is ready.
2) Preheat the oven to 350°F.
3) Place the croissants on a cookie sheet and cut them in half.
4) Boil the syrup for a few minutes and off the heat add the flavoring.
5) Spread the hot syrup inside and outside the croissants (if the croissants are not fresh use more syrup) and then spread the frangipane inside and on top. Sprinkle some sliced almonds on top and bake for about 15 minutes or until golden brown on top.
6) Serve sprinkled with powdered sugar.

Tips

If you have left over frangipane, you can keep it for several days in the fridge in an airtight container. You can use it at the bottom of fruit tarts or with puff pastry.

Galettes and Crepes
Galettes et Crêpes

Most cities in France have one or more crêperies -- restaurants that serve crepes from the first course to the last course. For entrées, very often buckwheat crepes, also called galettes are served stuffed with ham, cheese, eggs, mushrooms, onions, spinach, meats. For desserts, white flour crepes are stuffed with fruits, jams, chestnut spread --my favorite! -- ice-cream, sprinkled with nuts, drowned in liqueur, topped with pastry cream, coffee whipped cream or just sprinkled with sugar and flambéed with rum or brandy.

In the Limousin region, southwest of France, my Aunt Jeanne used to serve Tourtous, a buckwheat crepe that we used to eat like bread. It was eaten plain with soup for dinner or just spread with butter for dessert. We looked forward to having it every year during our visit in this region.

Brittany or Bretagne in French, located on the West coast of France, is where crepes originated. There are restaurants, bistros, food carts serving crepes cooked on a big cast iron circle. Some menus offer one hundred different varieties of crepes as thin as the lace on the folkloric hats worn by the Bretonnes ladies. These crepes are always served with a bowl of the local beverage, sparkling cider with a certain alcohol content.

In France, crepes are always associated with the Chandeleur a mid winter religious holiday held on February 2nd. Chandeleur, also called Candlemas is a celebration of light. In the pagan custom and Catholic religion candles were lit and round shaped crepes made representing the return of the sun, warmer days, and the coming prosperity of harvests.

We make a lot of crepes on that day, and as each member of the family flips them in a pan *with one hand, they have a gold coin in the other hand. If the crepe falls back into the pan, we will have money for the rest of the year. If it falls onto the stove or the floor, we will have financial problems.*

Buckwheat Crepes

Galettes or Tourtous: Crêpes au Sarrasin

These savory crepes can be filled with Chicken à la King, ham, broccoli, sautéed mushrooms, or spinach. All are topped with a mornay sauce. You can also use sausage or ground meats with a Marinara sauce or even ratatouille, a summer vegetable stew. Stuffed entrée crepes can be made a day ahead. They will keep better because the filling and the sauce will keep them from drying out.

Yields 10 to 12 thin 8 inches crepes   Intermediate

- 1 cup buckwheat flour (120 grams)
- ⅓ cup all-purpose white flour (42 grams)
- A pinch of salt
- 3 large eggs
- 1 cup milk
- ½ cup beer
- 2 tablespoons melted butter (28 grams)

Needed

- Mixing bowl
- Wooden spoon
- 8-inch nonstick pan or a de Buyer metal crepe pan
- Pastry brush
- Spatula or turner

1) Mix the flours and salt. Make a well in the center and add eggs.

2) Mix with a wooden spoon until it is a thick paste. Gradually add the beer then the milk. It should be the consistency of heavy cream.

3) Add the melted butter and rest at room temperature, covered with plastic wrap for 1 hour.

4) When ready to make crepes, stir batter and add more beer if too thick. The batter should be thin and fluid.

5) A small nonstick pan is perfect for the job. Use a brush to oil the pan lightly. You can use margarine, or oil but not olive oil. Use medium high heat.

6) When the pan is hot and the oil is shimmering throw a little cold water on the oil to see if it sizzles, take it off the heat and pour about ¼ to ⅓ cup of batter swirling it around the pan so it quickly spreads very thin. You might not use the whole quantity. If there is not enough spreading on the pan, you can add a little more in the bare spots. After a while you will know what quantity to use in the pan you have.

7) Cook on the stove until bubbles form and when the edges become brown, run a spatula to detach the sides of the crepe. Flip over using your fingers or a spatula. Cook the other side for a shorter time, 1 minute at the most. The crepe is ready when the center is soft and the edges crispy.

8) Stack on a plate and keep warm in a 150°F oven covered with foil or a towel.

Tips

The buckwheat flour will make them thicker than regular crepes, so be sure to aim for extra thin as possible. If they are too thick they are not as good! The borders should be like lace.

Crepes With Cheese Sauce

If you are having company this is a good dish to make in advance. Having the crepes already prepared allows you to spend more time with your guests. Traditionally savory crepes are always made using the buckwheat crepe recipe. However, if you do not have buckwheat flour, you may also use the dessert recipe found on page 168. Just omit the vanilla and sugar.

Yields 2 cups of sauce   Intermediate

- ¼ stick of butter (28 grams)
- 2 tablespoons flour (16 grams)
- 1 ½ cup milk
- Grated nutmeg
- 1 ½ cup grated Gruyère cheese divided (200 grams total)
- Salt and pepper

Needed

- Saucepan
- Whisk
- 9x13 inch oven proof baking dish

1) Make a roux with the butter and flour. When the butter is hot and sizzling, add the flour. Keep stirring with a whisk and when foaming, pour the cold milk gradually. Continue whisking with a whisk and stir until the sauce thickens. Put half of the cheese and salt and pepper at the end since the cheese tastes salty—do not salt before you put the cheese, or it will be too salty.

2) Once the crepes or galettes are made ahead of time, you could choose a filling of cooked shredded chicken, chopped ham or sautéed mushrooms that you mix with half of the sauce. Fill the crepes, one at a time and roll them side by side in a buttered dish. Cover with the rest of the sauce and top with ½ of the reserved cheese.

3) Cover the dish, you can keep it in the fridge until ready to bake. You can bake it or broil it. Everything is cooked so it is just a question of reheating them. If you want au gratin crepes, put them under the broiler so the cheese melts and becomes golden brown. If you just want melted cheese, put it in a 325°F oven, covered with aluminum foil for 20 to 25 minutes.

Ham and Cheese Crepes

1) Make the crepes one at a time. As the crepe is cooking on the first side watch for the bubbles in the center and the brown edges on the sides. It is time to turn your crepe over.

2) When ready to cook on the other side, add a slice of ham or chopped ham and sprinkle with grated Gruyère cheese. Fold the crepe in half or in quarters to allow the cheese to melt. Transfer to a plate. It is ready to eat.

The same can be done with caramelized onions, sliced mushrooms, sliced cooked sausage and cheese.

Ratatouille Crepes

1) Make the crepe the same way as above and when the second side is cooked and ready, you can fill the crepe with the ratatouille found on page 149.

2) If you want you can fill the crepes with ratatouille, roll them up and place them in a buttered dish. You can use leftover ratatouille to pour over the filled crepes. Cover and keep warm in a 325°F oven.

Tips

Crepes are an effective way to use your leftovers. Do not be afraid to make them paper thin just like lace on the outer edges. See How to Fold Crepes page 172.

Main Dishes

Beef Burgundy 94

Vol au Vent 97

Easy Cassoulet 100

Shakshouka 104

Stuffed Mushrooms 106

Au Gratin Scallops 109

Fondue Burgundy Style 112

Cheese Fondue 115

French Cottage Pie 118

Potato Omelet 121

Limousin Pâté 123

Chicken with Cream and Olives 126

Bolognese Spaghetti Sauce 128

Stuffed Tomatoes and Potatoes 130

Provençal Tomatoes 133

Quiche Lorraine and Chicken Asparagus Quiche 135

Beef Burgundy

Boeuf bourguignon

Julia Child's recipe is very good but time consuming. Having received a new enamel cast iron Dutch oven from my daughter for a birthday, I had to make the boeuf bourguignon in it. This recipe is the one we use in Burgundy. Although it is served in winter, it can be eaten year-round. Delicious!

Serves 4 to 6   Easy

- ½ pound bacon chopped up (225 grams)
- 1 or 2 tablespoons safflower oil
- 2 pounds of sirloin tips cut into cubes and dried with a paper towel
- 2 or 3 medium yellow onions chopped or small pearl onions (about ¼ pound)
- 1 tablespoon flour (7 grams)
- ½ to ¾ quart of table red wine
- 1 head garlic with about 10 to 15 cloves

- 1 medium carrot
- 1 bouquet garni made from 1 bay leaf, 1 branch of thyme, 1 branch parsley tied with string to ease removal. Or use 1 teaspoon each of dried herbs.
- 1 tablespoon tomato paste
- 2 or 3 tablespoons butter (28 to 43 grams)
- ½ pound mushrooms (225 grams)
- Minced parsley for garnish
- Baguette slices brushed with olive oil, toasted at 400°F for 3 or 4 minutes then rubbed with garlic
- Salt and pepper

Needed

- Enamel cast iron Dutch oven
- Chef's knife
- Wooden spoon
- Small frying pan

1) Sauté the bacon in the Dutch oven. When golden and browned, remove from the pot and save.

2) In the same pot, add 1 or 2 tablespoons of oil to the bacon fat, and when it sizzles, sauté the meat in portions so it browns easily. If you cook the meat cubes all together, they will render too much juice and the meat will not brown. When all the meat is browned, add the onions. Add salt and pepper.

3) Once the meat and onions are browned, add the flour and mix, then add the red wine.

4) Slice the carrot, chop the cloves of garlic, and prepare the bouquet garni.

5) Add all these to the pot with the tomato paste. Adjust the seasoning. Mix and let simmer for at least 1 hour and 30 minutes or until the meat is tender. If you have an InstaPot you can use the stew function of the pressure cooker program for 45 minutes.

6) Slice the mushrooms and sauté them in a frying pan with a little butter. Add salt and pepper.

7) Before serving, add the bacon and the mushrooms.

8) Serve with steamed or mashed potatoes and baguette slices toasted then rubbed with garlic. Garnish with a sprinkling of chopped parsley.

Vol au Vent
Bouchées à la Reine

My dad enjoyed making this simple dish that looks like a lot of work but with premade puff pastry dough it is not.

In France, we often make them with sweetbreads, which are the thymus of the calf. This was a delicacy in a lot of restaurants. It is a delicate puff pastry served with chopped up cooked chicken, ham, mushrooms, seafood or even foie gras in a thick white sauce.

Nicolas Stohrer created this dish, in honor of Louis XV's wife, Marie Leszczynska, (1703-1768) a Polish princess and queen of France - La reine. It was supposed to have aphrodisiac virtues! It is also called Vol au Vent because the pastry is so light it can "fly in the wind."

Serves 4   Intermediate

- 4 frozen pastry shells preferably from a brand the uses real butter
- 1 tablespoon safflower oil
- 10 button mushrooms, cleaned and cut in quarters
- Salt and pepper for the mushrooms

- 2 cups cooked chicken seasoned with salt and pepper, or cubed shrimp, crab, scallops (270 grams)
- 2 tablespoons butter (28 grams)
- 2 tablespoons flour (16 grams)
- 1¼ cup half and half
- ¼ cup dry white wine
- Salt and pepper to taste
- ⅛ teaspoon ground nutmeg
- ½ cup shredded Gruyère cheese (optional)

Needed

- Cookie sheet
- Paring knife
- Frying pan
- Wooden spoon or spatula
- Plate
- Saucepan
- Whisk
- Grater

1) Preheat the oven to 425°F.
2) Bake the frozen shells in the oven for about 18 to 20 minutes according to the package directions. When baked, use the tip of a knife to remove the little lid in the middle of each pastry shell.
3) In a little oil, sauté the mushrooms until lightly golden. Add salt and pepper. When done, place them aside on a plate.
4) Make a béchamel sauce using the butter. When the butter sizzles, pour all the flour. Cook for about 2 to 3 minutes. When the mixture foams, slowly pour the cold half and half. Whisk constantly with a whisk until the mix-

ture thickens gradually. The whisking will prevent lumps in the sauce. Mix well and add the white wine. You will have a thick and smooth sauce. Add salt and pepper to your taste and grate some nutmeg for flavor.

5) Reheat the shells in a 300°F oven if necessary for 5 to 6 minutes in the oven.

6) Place the cooked mushrooms and the meat cut in cubes in the sauce. Let the whole mixture simmer for 5 minutes. Adjust seasoning.

7) Pour the warm sauce in the pastry shells and serve warm.

Tips

If your sauce is too runny you can thicken with grated cheese or serve separately.

This would be a great way to serve as a substitute to chicken or turkey pot pie when you have holiday leftovers.

Easy Cassoulet

Cassoulet

This is a peasant winter dish and one of the most complete meals. It is a favorite during the holidays at our house. The name comes from cassolette which means a big earthen pot to cook a bean dish. It dates to the 12th century. Cassoulet was served to the French soldiers to sustain them during the Hundred Years War against the British in the 14th century.

There is a cassoulet from Toulouse, one from Castelnaudary and one from Carcassone, all cities in the Occitanie region, in southern France. Each one has different meats in the traditional bean dish. Each city claims theirs is the best!

Cassoulet is a dish that can be cooked for a long time.

After several hours of cooking, a crust is supposed to form on top of the cassoulet. Every hour or so, a ladle of broth is added while pushing down the crust. Most of the connoisseurs would not eat cassoulet unless it has been reheated 4 or 5 times so the flavors infuse the whole dish!

The cassoulet of the rich would have confit d'oie -- goose parts cooked in goose fat and salt-- while the cassoulet of the poor would include sausages, chicken, or lamb.

So be creative! .Make your own recipe by adding lamb chops, cubed pork tenderloin, smoked pork chops if you have less than an hour to cook. Add cubed pork shoulder, lamb shanks, pork shanks, chicken thighs, bacon, sausages if you have more than 2 hours to cook.

Serves 6 to 8   Easy

- 4 slices of bacon cut in 2 inches chunks
- 2 pounds chicken thighs (900 grams)
- 1 or 2 tablespoons margarine or butter (14 to 28 grams)
- 1 pound flavorful but not spicy sausage cut in chunks (450 grams)
- 2 tablespoons margarine or oil
- 1 medium chopped onion
- 1 chopped celery stick
- 3 chopped carrots
- 4 minced cloves of garlic
- 4 15 ounce cans of white beans
- 2 tablespoons tomato paste or 2 chopped up fresh tomatoes
- 1 cup chicken broth
- 1 bouquet garni made from 1 bay leaf, 1 branch of thyme, 1 branch parsley tied with string to ease removal. Or use 1 teaspoon each of dried herbs.
- 2 teaspoon salt
- 1 teaspoon pepper

Needed

- Frying pan or skillet
- Chef's knife
- Cast iron 4 to 5 quart Dutch oven, preferably enamel.

One hour and a half before dinner

1) Fry the bacon until brown and crisp on medium high heat. Remove to paper towel, Reserve the bacon fat in a bowl for later.

2) In the same pot/skillet, put 1 tablespoon of margarine or oil and add the chicken pieces while hot. Sprinkle with ½ teaspoon of salt and ¼ teaspoon of pepper. Sauté until brown on each side about 20 to 30 minutes. When the chicken is golden brown, set aside.

3) Cook the sausage chunks in the same pot/skillet. Add ½ teaspoon salt and ¼ teaspoon of the pepper. Once cooked, set them aside on a plate.

One hour before dinner

4) Preheat oven to 400°F.

5) Chop the vegetables and mince the garlic. Add 1 tablespoon of margarine or oil in the same pot/skillet you cooked the meat in and sauté the vegetables until limp and tender on medium high heat, about 5 to 10 minutes.

6) Mix in the tomato paste or tomatoes. Reduce the heat to simmer and mix in 1 cup of chicken broth, the bouquet garni, ½ teaspoon of salt and ¼ teaspoon of pepper and simmer for 5 minutes.

7) Drain the beans and add them to the pot/skillet. Mix with the remaining ½ teaspoon of salt and ¼ teaspoon of pepper. Simmer covered for 5 minutes.

8) Drizzle half of the bacon fat at the bottom of a 4 to 5-quart Dutch oven-- like Le Creuset or Staub. Layer a third of the bean mixture, then the bacon and sausage another third of the beans, then the chicken pieces and the last third of the bean mixture. Drizzle the remaining leftover bacon fat on top.

9) Cover the Dutch oven and bake for 30 minutes. Uncover and bake for at least another 30 minutes. If it gets dry, add more broth. Before serving make sure you remove the bouquet garni and adjust seasoning again if you added more broth assuming it is not salted broth.

10) Serve with minced parsley.

Tips

Over the years, I have cut down on the time soaking beans, by using 15 ounce cans of Navy beans or Great Northern beans. Do not stir the cassoulet!

The purists will tell you that the real cassoulet does not need breadcrumbs. The crust will be formed on top of the cassoulet naturally. You keep adding bouillon by pushing on the crusty beans and moistening the whole dish at least 7 times during the cooking process.

In the Toulouse area, they like to sprinkle breadcrumbs on top to make like a gratinée!

Shakshouka

Chakchouka

Shakshouka is a Tunisian and Israeli specialty made with tomatoes, onions, peppers, spices, and eggs. It is eaten for breakfast or lunch, and it is so easy to make!! It is like a Turkish dish called Menemen or Huevos Rancheros in Latin America. This is an adaptation of a recipe from my French friend from grade school in Autun, Laure Pauchard.

Serves 4   Easy

- 1 or 2 tablespoons olive oil
- 1 medium onion diced
- 3 colorful medium peppers diced (red, orange, yellow)
- 3 large cloves of garlic minced
- 3 or 4 medium tomatoes chopped
- 1 teaspoon cumin
- ½ teaspoon paprika
- ¼ teaspoon cayenne pepper

- Salt to taste
- 4 large eggs

Needed

- Large frying pan
- Mixing bowl
- A spatula or wooden spoon

1) Combine the tomatoes, the cumin, paprika, salt and cayenne pepper in a bowl and mix rapidly together.

2) Heat the olive oil in a frying pan on medium heat. Add the onion, peppers, and cook for 5 to 6 minutes until all the vegetables are soft and translucent. Add garlic and cook until fragrant about 30 seconds,

3) Pour in the tomato mixture and cook for 10 minutes with the lid off until all the liquid has evaporated.

4) Make 4 holes in that mixture and break one egg in each hole. Cover the frying pan and let the eggs poach until cooked but not hard (about 5 minutes). Watch carefully as it is easy to overcook the eggs. Cook the eggs to your liking adding a little salt and pepper on top.

Stuffed Mushrooms

Champignons farcis

The Limousin area in southwest France is renowned for its mushrooms and truffles. Together with my parents, aunt, and uncle I spent a lot of vacation time hunting for chanterelles and boletus. When the season was good, we had so many that we fixed them in omelets, or as an accompaniment for a meat. Those we could not eat fresh were preserved by drying on a rack. As kids we loved to watch the worms fall off the mushrooms as they dried out!

Here is a recipe from Limousin for stuffed boletus. You can also use Portobello mushrooms.

Serves 4   Easy

- 4 big heads of boletus or Portobello mushrooms
- 1 tablespoon olive oil
- 1 tablespoon butter
- 3 medium shallots minced
- 1 clove garlic minced

- ½ pound ground pork or beef (225 grams)
- ¼ cup parsley chopped
- 1 large egg
- 1 teaspoon dried thyme
- 1 teaspoon salt and ½ teaspoon pepper combined
- 1 or two slices white bread soaked in broth or water and squeezed out (optional)
- 4 tablespoons breadcrumbs
- 2 tablespoons of butter

Needed
- Paring knife
- Chef's knife
- Frying pan
- Mixing bowl
- Measuring spoons
- An ovenproof 9x13 baking dish

1) Mushrooms should not be soaked in water. Brush clean or wipe with a damp cloth. Separate the stems from the heads. Chop the stems. Remove the gills by scraping with a spoon to create more space for filling.

2) In a frying pan, first sauté the mushroom heads in the oil. Add ⅓ of the quantity of salt and pepper. mixture. When they are golden, flip them over and cook the other side then place them in the baking dish.

3) In the same frying pan, add the butter and sauté the chopped stems, the shallots, and the garlic. Add another ⅓ of the salt and pepper. Cook for 10 to 15 minutes on medium heat.

4) Preheat the oven to 400°F.

5) Mix the pork with the chopped parsley, the egg, the thyme, add the re-

maining salt and pepper. If you want to add the moist bread at this point, it will make the stuffing lighter.

6) Add the cooked items to the stuffing and mix well. Stuff each mushroom with pork filling, sprinkling a tablespoon of breadcrumbs per mushroom on top of the filling. Add half a tablespoon of butter on each top.

7) Place the mushrooms into a baking dish and bake for about 30-35 minutes.

Tips

You can serve this dish by itself or with purée de pommes de terre – mashed potatoes, rice, or a green salad.

You may want to add shredded cheese instead of breadcrumbs, this is your choice. Be creative!

In the Limousin region, they also use chopped smoked ham instead of ground pork.

Au Gratin Scallops
Coquilles Saint-Jacques au gratin

This is one of my favorite dishes at home. You can find the scallops shells in any cooking or gourmet stores but also in large supermarkets. It is a spectacular dish and a treat for every guest, especially when served in the scallop shell.

It is called coquilles saint Jacques in French because when pilgrims on the road to Saint Jacques de Compostelle, arrived in the North of Spain, they would pick up these shells on the beach and attach them to their backpacks or clothes for good luck and as testimony that they arrived at their destination.

In the US, we only eat the white part of the scallop, but in France they eat both the white part and orange part, le corail, which has a great flavor.

Serves 4   Intermediate

- 8 large or 12 medium size scallops
- 1 cup of table white wine
- 2 medium minced shallots
- 1 tablespoons of butter (14 grams)
- 1 cup of sliced button mushrooms (150 grams)
- 1 bouquet garni made from 1 bay leaf, 1 branch of thyme, 1 branch parsley tied with string to ease removal. Or use 1 teaspoon each of dried herbs.
- The juice of ½ a lemon – about 2 tablespoons (optional)
- Salt and pepper to taste

White sauce

- 1 tablespoon of butter (14 grams)

- 1 tablespoon of flour (7 grams)
- ¾ cup of the bouillon from the scallops
- 1 cup of shredded Gruyère cheese (110 grams)
- Salt and pepper to taste
- Breadcrumbs

Needed

- Deep skillet
- Medium size saucepan
- Fine mesh sieve
- Whisk
- 4 Scallop shells or ramequins
- A broiling pan or cookie sheet

1) In a skillet bring to a boil the white wine, the shallots, butter, bouquet garni, salt and pepper, and reduce heat to a simmer for 5 minutes.

2) Brush the mushrooms clean and slice them or cut them in quarters. Sprinkle with lemon if you want. Add them to the bouillon. Simmer for 5 minutes. Add the scallops in the last 2 minutes. Remove mushrooms and scallops and strain through a fine mesh sieve reserving ¾ cup of the bouillon.

3) Turn the oven on broil.

4) Make the white sauce by melting the butter in a saucepan. When sizzling, add the flour and when the mixture is foaming, slowly add the reserved bouillon while whisking until it thickens. Simmer for 5 minutes. Taste and adjust salt and pepper remembering that the cheese will give a salty flavor also.

5) Butter scallop shells or ramequins. Evenly divide the scallop/mushroom mixture into each shell or ramequin, allowing about 2 to 3 scallops per shell or dish depending on the size. Cover with the white sauce.

6) Sprinkle each dish with shredded Gruyère and breadcrumbs.

7) Place under the broiler and watch closely. Remove when cheese and breadcrumbs are golden brown.

Tips

You can prepare everything ahead of time up until it is time to fill the shells. At the last minute, fill the shells and broil for a few minutes.

It can be served as a main course or as a first course in a banquet or for a special occasion luncheon. As a main course serve with the white molded rice which can be found on page 142.

Fondue Burgundy Style
Fondue bourguignonne

Growing up in Burgundy, this was a staple at our house, many weekends. My mom would buy the sauce readymade, but my dad would try to always make some homemade sauces.

You can also have vegetables to fry beside the meat for vegetarian options.

Serves 4 to 6   Easy

- 1 ½ pound beef top sirloin or tenderloin (750 grams)
- 2 cups safflower or peanut oil
- An assortment of Dijon mustards, plain or in grains, like Maille, Grey Poupon, Fallot
- Cornichons or small pickles
- Capers
- Ketchup
- Various sauces like premade sauces: chili sauce, mustard sauce, mayonnaise, aioli, tartar (see below for homemade sauces)

- Chips, steamed potatoes, and a green salad as accompaniments

Needed

- ➤ Fondue pot with a burner or electric fondue pot
- ➤ 4 long fondue forks
- ➤ 4 plates and silverware

1) Cut the raw meat in cubes. Place them on each guest's plate.
2) Place the condiments and sauces in separate bowls or on each guest plate.
3) The fondue pot should be ⅔ full of oil. When the oil is hot at about 375°F, place a piece of meat on a long fondue fork and let it fry.
4) When cooked, place the meat in your plate and with a different fork, dip it in the sauce and eat it with some condiments.
5) You can eat with a green salad or chips or even steamed potatoes.

Mayonnaise

- 1 large egg yolk at room temperature
- ½ tablespoon Dijon mustard at room temperature
- ½ tablespoon white, cider, or wine vinegar
- Salt and pepper
- ⅓ to ½ cup extra virgin olive oil, safflower, peanut, or corn oil
- At the end: 1 teaspoon vinegar and 1 tablespoon boiling water

Needed

- ➤ Stand or handheld mixer or food processor
- ➤ Medium mixing bowl

1) Mix the first three ingredients beating at medium high speed.

2) When the mixture is smooth and well blended, add the oil in a trickle until the mayonnaise starts to thicken and take shape. Keep beating at high speed the whole time. At this point you can pour the oil in a bigger stream.

3) When the mayonnaise is set, you can add 1 teaspoon of vinegar and/or a teaspoon of boiling water to make the sauce lighter and hold better.

4) Add salt and pepper to taste.

Tips

If your mayonnaise failed, do not throw it away! Start over with an egg yolk, mustard and vinegar, salt and pepper and slowly trickle in the failed mixture. If you need to add a little oil afterwards, go ahead.

Aioli

- 6 cloves of minced garlic

1) Make the mayonnaise as above, following the same conditions and instructions.

2) Add the minced garlic to the mayonnaise

Tartar

- 1 teaspoon vinegar
- 1 minced shallot
- 2 teaspoons capers
- 4 to 5 minced cornichons or pickles
- Parsley, chives, chervil, tarragon minced

1) Follow the mayonnaise directions and at the end, add the vinegar, shallot, capers, minced pickles, and the minced herbs. Mix well in the sauce.

Cheese Fondue

Fondue savoyarde

Fondue is a classic in Switzerland and the French Alps where we have spent many vacations. It is an excuse to eat melted cheese and have a convivial meal with family or friends. It is a favorite of our whole family in the winter and especially around Christmas and New Year. Our daughter likes to add cut up broccoli or cauliflower for a healthy fondue!

Very often in Savoie and Haute-Savoie, they serve it with pickles, cornichons, smoked meats like ham, sausages or even with boiled potatoes in their jackets.

The etiquette is to use the fondue fork for anchoring and dipping the bread in the melted cheese. Using a knife, you then slide the cheesy bread onto your plate and use a different fork to eat it.

If anyone drops his/her bread in the cheese, he or she will buy a bottle of Savoie wine or host the next fondue party!

At the end, you can break an egg in the remaining melted crispy cheese and make an omelet that you can share with everyone.

Serves 4 to 6   Easy

- 1 garlic clove sliced in half horizontally
- 1 cup dry white wine
- 1 pound grated cheese Comté, Emmenthal, Gruyère if made in the US. In Savoie they use Comté, Gruyère, Beaufort, Abondance (450 grams)
- A baguette or a loaf of French bread cut into 1-inch cubes
- 2 teaspoons cornstarch (5 grams)
- 2 pinches of grated nutmeg
- 4 tablespoons kirsch or brandy
- Fresh ground black pepper
- 2 pinches of baking soda

Needed:

- Enamel cast iron fondue set with a burner like Le Creuset
- Cheese grater
- Measuring cups and spoons or a scale
- Nutmeg grater
- Medium bowl
- Wooden spoon
- Peppermill

1) Rub the fondue pot with the garlic. Add the wine and heat on the stove until it bubbles. Do not let it boil.

2) Toss the cheese with the cornstarch and the nutmeg in a bowl. Add grated cheese mixture a handful at a time in the hot wine. Cook over low heat until the cheese is melted and smooth. Use a wooden spoon to stir constantly.

3) Stir in the kirsch and the black pepper and baking soda.

4) Light the burner under the fondue pot and set it on medium. If the cheese starts to bubble, lower to the low setting.

5) Enjoy a convivial meal that you set in the middle of the table.

Tips

The sodium bicarbonate of the baking soda helps make the fondue easier to digest.

The cornstarch helps to thicken the mixture and prevents it from turning sour. If this happens it can be remedied with a drop of vinegar.

Usually, we count about 150 grams to 200 grams of cheese per person.

French Cottage Pie

Hachis Parmentier

Hachis Parmentier was a classic at our house, but I adapted it over the years. My mom used to make it when she had left-over roast or beef stew and my dad used to grind the meat, cranking the grinder manually, to put it in the Hachis Parmentier.

Antoine-Augustin Parmentier was a French Army pharmacist, agronomist and nutritionist who believed potatoes were a great food source because of their nutritional value: it would prevent famine, in France and Europe in the 18th century, under King Louis XVI. Until then, potatoes were used as animal feed and were considered toxic to humans, even causing leprosy! He founded a school of breadmaking (using potato flour to make bread during a famine). He also studied refrigeration as a means of conserving food.

His tomb is in Paris in the Père Lachaise Cemetery. It is surrounded by potato plants. His name is also on a Paris subway station and a Paris avenue in the 10th and 11th arrondissements.

Anything called Parmentier, in French, means it includes potatoes.

Serves 6 to 8   Intermediate

Mashed potatoes:

- 5 or 6 large potatoes
- 2 tablespoons butter (28 grams)
- 1 cup whole milk or whipping cream
- Salt and pepper
- Grated nutmeg
- 1 cup to 1½ cup shredded Gruyère or Comté cheese (250 to 375 grams)
- Breadcrumbs or Panko

Meat mixture:

- 1 pound ground beef or lamb (450 to 500 grams)
- 1 box of Mirepoix, about 15 ounces, or 1 large onion diced, 3 medium size carrots diced, and 2 medium size celery branches diced
- Herbes de Provence
- 1 chopped garlic clove
- Salt and pepper
- 1 tablespoon tomato paste (16 grams)
- 1 tablespoon flour (7 grams)
- 1 to 1½ cup beef broth
- 1 cup frozen peas (160 grams)

Needed

- Saucepan
- Potato masher
- Frying pan
- 9x13 baking dish

1) Preheat the oven to 400°F.
2) Cook the potatoes in water. Mash the potatoes with butter and warm milk or whipping cream. Add salt, pepper, and grated nutmeg. Add ½ cup of the shredded cheese.
3) In a frying pan, sauté the ground meat on medium heat until completely cooked. Add the mirepoix, chopped garlic and Herbes de Provence. Cook until the vegetables are soft. Add salt and pepper.
4) Add the tomato paste and mix well. Add the flour and mix well.
5) When everything is simmering add 1 to 1 ½ cup of broth while stirring well so the liquid is mostly absorbed by the flour and the tomato paste. If it is too liquid, turn the heat to medium high and wait till most of the

liquid is evaporated. The mixture should be moist and not dry.

6) Add the peas and adjust the seasoning.

7) In a buttered 9x13 baking dish, layer the meat mixture and on top place the mashed potatoes mixture.

8) Cover with the remaining shredded cheese and the breadcrumbs or Panko.

9) Bake for 20 to 25 minutes or until the top is brown and sizzling.

Potato Omelet
Omelette Parmentier

As I mentioned in the Hachis Parmentier recipe, any dish called Parmentier means it includes potatoes.

Most recipes for this dish ask for boiled potatoes but Mamie Gisèle and I thought the omelet is better when you fry raw potatoes. The potatoes are crispier. This was a classic at our house for dinners.

Serve 4 to 6   Easy

- 1½ tablespoons unsalted butter (21 grams)
- 1½ tablespoons safflower oil
- 1½ pound Yukon Gold potatoes (675 grams)
- Salt and pepper
- 5 large eggs beaten
- Chives or chopped parsley as a garnish- (optional)

Needed

- Medium size frying pan-10 inch
- Medium size mixing bowl
- Metal spatula
- Fork
- Round serving platter, a little bigger than the frying pan

1) Melt the butter and oil in a frying pan. Peel and slice the potatoes, pat dry, and add to the frying pan. Add salt and pepper. After several minutes turn them over so they cook and brown evenly.
2) When they are browned on both sides, add the beaten eggs, and cook on medium high heat, lifting the potatoes with spatula so the egg runs under the potatoes.
3) When the omelet is dry on the sides and a little moist in the center, take a round serving platter, turn it over the pan and flip the pan so the omelet is served flat on the dish.
4) If you want, sprinkle some chopped parsley or chives on top before serving.

Tips

You can add some bacon or some chopped onions when frying the potatoes.

You can increase the quantity of potatoes and eggs according to the number of guests you have.

Limousin Pâté

Pâté Limousin

In July 2009, I was with my mom visiting the Musée Jacques Chirac in Sarran, a village in the département of Corrèze, in the Limousin region. This is where I enjoyed a Pâté Corrézien also called Pâté Limousin. It just melted in my mouth. This is the version I made once I got home!

Jacques Chirac's presidential library is in this village to honor his parents and grandparents and because it was where he began a political career that would take him from president of the Corrèze General Council to Prime Minister of France, Mayor of Paris, and finally President of France from 1995 to 2007.

After we admired the museum and its impressive display of gifts he had received from famous heads of state, my mom and I had lunch in the attached restaurant. To our surprise and delight President Chirac, his daughter, and his bodyguards were having lunch at a table next to us. Following lunch, he agreed to have a picture taken with me. This was a memorable day for us.

Serves 8 to 10   Easy

- 2 sheets of frozen puff pastry preferably made with butter
- 8 large baking potatoes about 2 pounds (900 grams)

- 1 pound sweet Italian ground pork (450 grams)
- 1 bunch of curly parsley chopped
- 6 cloves of garlic minced
- ¾ cup crème fraiche or sour cream (140 grams)
- Salt and pepper
- 1 egg yolk

Needed

- 9x13 glass baking dish greased
- Rolling pin
- Paring knife
- Food processor
- Medium mixing bowl
- Small mixing bowl
- Pastry brush

1) Use a 9x13 glass dish that has been greased with butter or oil.
2) Preheat oven to 410°F.
3) Roll out the first sheet of dough so it is 12x14, leaving an overlap over the glass dish.
4) Slice the potatoes thinly and mix with the cream. Add salt and pepper generously. Place half the potatoes on the dough.
5) In a food processor, chop the parsley and garlic. Mix in a medium mixing bowl with the ground pork. Salt and pepper. Place the pork mixture on top of the potatoes.
6) Top with the remaining half of the potatoes. Salt and pepper.
7) Roll the second sheet of dough to 9x13 and place it on top of the potatoes.
8) Beat one egg with 1 tablespoon of water. Brush this mixture on the over-

laps of the dough so it acts as glue, overlapping the bottom dough over the top dough all around the sides. Make sure you brush all the dough exposed with the remainder of the egg wash, so it browns better.

9) Make 3 or 4 little holes on top of the dough so that the steam escapes while baking.

10) Put in the oven and bake for 45 minutes.

Tips

This is a great main dish with a salad.

Former President Jacques Chirac and myself

Chicken with Cream and Olives

Poulet aux olives

This was a regular at our house for Sunday lunch.

Serves 4 to 6   Easy

- One chicken cut up or the equivalent in chicken pieces like thighs, breasts or legs with skin removed

- 2 bacon slices chopped in 1-inch pieces

- ⅛ cup of Cognac or Armagnac or other alcohol you have on hand

- French tarragon or French thyme, fresh if possible and use one or the other as much as you want

- 1 medium chopped onion or shallots

- 4 ounce green olives Spanish or California

- ½ pint heavy cream, half and half or crème fraiche -- make your own by bringing 1 cup of whipping cream and 1 tablespoon of sour cream to 90/100°F and then leave it on the counter overnight and refrigerate up to 2 weeks

- 1 egg yolk
- Salt and pepper to taste
- Chopped parsley for garnish
- Quartered mushrooms or sliced mushrooms (optional)

Needed

- Frying pan
- Small mixing bowl
- Serving platter

1) Sauté the bacon pieces until light brown in a pan or a Dutch oven. Add the chicken pieces and cook until brown on all sides but not cooked through, about 15 minutes. Add salt and pepper.

2) Flambé with Cognac or brandy. The Cognac must be a little warm before it catches fire.

3) Add the tarragon or thyme and the chopped onion or shallots.

4) If the olives are too salty, rinse them a little. Add the olives, if you decided to add mushrooms, you can add them at this time too. Cover and cook for about 30 minutes on medium low. Check the seasoning.

5) Take the chicken out of the pan or Dutch oven and keep it warm, covered in the oven at 200°F. Mix the egg yolk and the cream in a bowl; if you use crème fraîche, you get a thicker and creamier sauce. Mix in with the pan juices on low heat. Stir until the sauce thickens but make sure it does not boil.

6) Check the final seasonings. Pour the sauce over the chicken. Decorate with chopped parsley. Serve with molded rice as a fancy addition, arranged around the chicken platter. See recipe for molded rice on page 142.

Tips

Make sure you cook the egg yolk and cream at low heat, or the mixture will separate and curdle!

Bolognese Spaghetti Sauce

Sauce spaghetti à la bolognaise

My mom, Mamie Gisèle, often cooked pasta when we were kids, but it has never been one of my favorite dishes. When I moved to the USA and was married, my family enjoyed a great Italian pasta dish so I got busy concocting a Bolognese sauce that would please my family and finally me. There it is!!

Our daughter retrieved it in her archives since I do not use a recipe for it. When she goes to Russia, she makes that sauce on a regular basis for her crew.

Serves 6 to 8   Easy

- 1 pound ground beef (450 grams) or ¾ pound ground beef and ¼ pound ground pork (340 grams and 113 grams)
- ⅛ cup olive oil
- 1½ cloves of garlic minced
- 15 ounces mirepoix made with 1 medium onion diced, 2 carrots diced, and 2 celery sticks diced (425 grams)
- 2 15 ounce cans chopped tomatoes (850 grams)
- 1-6 ounce can tomato paste (170 grams)
- 1- 8 ounce can tomato sauce (227 grams)
- 2 tablespoons grated Romano cheese (10 grams)
- 1½ cup red wine
- Herbes de Provence to taste
- 1 bay leaf
- Salt and pepper to taste

Needed

- Large cooking pot
- Wooden spoon
- Paring knife
- Chef's knife

1) Sauté the ground meat on medium heat until all cooked. Drain the fat. Add the mirepoix and the minced garlic. Cook for about 5 minutes until the onions are translucent.

2) Add the chopped tomatoes, the tomato paste, and the tomato sauce. Stir well.

3) Add the Romano cheese. Stir well. It will be thick.

4) Add one cup of wine and see how much thinner the sauce becomes..

5) Add the Herbes de Provence, bay leaf, salt, and pepper.

6) Let simmer covered for 1 or 2 hours. The longer you cook it the better. If you want the sauce a little thicker take the lid off in the last 30 minutes. If it gets too thick you can add that last ½ cup of wine.

Tips

This sauce can be used with any pasta: spaghetti, fettucine, lasagna, raviolis, tortellini.

You can add sauteed mushrooms to this sauce if you want.

Even though most of the alcohol evaporates while cooking, the flavor might be strong for children. If that is the case, you can substitute beef broth or vegetable broth.

Mangia! Buon Appetito!

Stuffed Tomatoes and Potatoes
Tomates et pommes de terre farcies

Every summer, my mom, Mamie Gisèle, used to make this dish for our lunch. It was delicious! She often used leftover roast that my dad would grind by hand. You can also use fresh ground meat. I have had it with beef and pork, and they are equally scrumptious. Mamie Gisèle would slice some potatoes to put under the stuffed tomatoes to soak up the juices. They melted in your mouth.

Serves 6 to 8   Intermediate

- 4 large tomatoes
- 4 large Yukon Gold potatoes
- ½ cup of day old sandwich bread (100grams)
- ½ cup of milk
- 5 or 6 sprigs of parsley minced
- 1 medium onion minced
- 2 large garlic cloves minced

- ¾ pound ground beef or pork cooked or not (340 grams)
- 1 egg
- ⅓ cup breadcrumbs (50 grams)
- 2 tablespoons of butter (28 grams)
- Salt and pepper to taste
- 1 tablespoon Herbes de Provence

Needed

- Paring knife
- Chef's knife
- Teaspoon
- Small bowl
- Medium mixing bowl
- Large baking dish

1) Preheat oven to 375°F.

2) Cut a lid in the top of the tomatoes, right below the stem which has been removed. Save the lids for later. With a teaspoon empty the inside of the tomato without piercing the skin. Save the pulp and juice. Salt and pepper the inside generously and turn them upside down to drain them while you are preparing the stuffing.

3) Cut a lid in the potatoes and empty out most of the inside with a knife. Salt and pepper the inside generously. Save the lids for later.

4) Tear the bread into 1-inch pieces and soak with milk in a small bowl until soft but still holding its shape. Squeeze the milk out of the bread and place it in a medium bowl.

5) Mix bread with the ground meat, egg, minced parsley, onion, garlic, salt, pepper, and some of the tomato juice if the mixture is a little dry. Mix well.

6) Stuff the tomatoes and the potatoes with the meat stuffing.

7) Butter a baking dish. Place the tomatoes and potatoes in the dish. Sprinkle the breadcrumbs on top of each. Place ½ tablespoon of butter on top of each.

8) Bake for 30 minutes. After 30 minutes replace the lids on each vegetable and cook for another 30 minutes.

Tips

You could slice some extra potatoes and place them under the tomatoes and potatoes to soak up the juices too. A particularly good flavor.

Provençal Tomatoes
Tomates Provençales

This is a lighter vegan version of the Tomates et pommes de terre farcies/Stuffed Tomatoes and Potatoes.

Serves 4 to 6   Easy

- 4 large tomatoes
- 1 tablespoon butter
- 4 cloves of garlic minced
- ¼ cup chopped parsley
- 3 tablespoons of breadcrumbs
- 2 tablespoons butter (½ tablespoon per tomato)
- Salt and pepper

Needed

- Paring knife
- Chef's knife
- Frying pan
- Tongs
- 9x13 baking dish (optional)

1) Cut the tomatoes in half, remove the stem end and salt them, turning them upside down to drain while you are preparing the stuffing.

2) In a frying pan melt 1 tablespoon of butter and place the tomatoes on the cut side. Cook 2 minutes on medium heat then turn them over and cook another 2 minutes. Add salt and pepper.

3) Mix the minced garlic, chopped parsley and the breadcrumbs, salt and pepper. Place this on top of the cut side of the tomatoes.

4) Add ½ tablespoon butter on top of each tomato and let simmer on medium heat, covered for at least 10 minutes. You can also do this step in a 400°F oven by placing the tomatoes in a buttered baking dish and cook for 20 minutes or until the breadcrumbs are golden.

5) Serve with pork or veal cutlets, beef steaks, or with scrambled eggs.

Quiche Lorraine and Chicken Asparagus Quiche
Quiche Lorraine and Quiche poulet et asperges

A quiche is a French type of pie usually filled with chopped bacon, cheese in a mixture of eggs and cream. This is named for the region of Lorraine, in the northeast part of France.

I usually make quiches when I have leftover meat and vegetables. I think of it as the French equivalent to the Italian pizza. You can make your own crust or buy a prepared crust.

You can make a quiche with cooked mushrooms and onions, salmon and broccoli, chicken and artichoke hearts, ham and cheese, the choices are endless! You mix 3 or 4 eggs, some cream and shredded cheese, pour it over and you have a hearty quiche and a quick meal!

I have also made crustless quiches when I am too lazy or pressed for time to make a crust. It works too!

Yield one 10-inch regular or a 9-inch deep dish quiche.

Serves 6 to 8   Intermediate

Pastry

- 1 cup white all-purpose flour (120 grams)

- ¼ teaspoon salt
- ⅓ cup cut up unsalted chilled butter (79 grams)
- 1 large egg
- 1 tablespoon iced water
- 1 teaspoon lemon juice

Needed

- 10-inch quiche pan or a 9-inch-deep dish mold buttered
- 3 medium mixing bowls
- Pastry blender
- Rolling pin
- Plastic wrap

1) Preheat the oven to 400°F.
2) Stir the flour and the salt in a bowl. With the pastry blender, mix the pieces of butter in the flour until it resembles cornmeal.
3) In another bowl, mix the egg, lemon, and water. Sprinkle over the flour. Toss with a fork and gather in a ball. Wrap it airtight and leave it in the freezer about 10 minutes.
4) On a lightly floured work surface roll out the dough with a rolling pin, in a circle to fit your mold. It should be 1 inch larger than the mold. Fold the dough in quarters to place in the mold. Unfold and press to fit.

Quiche Lorraine

- 3 or 4 bacon slices cooked and crumbled, or 2 ham slices cut up
- 1 small shallot minced and cooked
- 3 to 4 large eggs
- ¾ to 1 cup whipping cream

- 1 cup shredded Swiss or Gruyère cheese (110 grams)
- Salt and pepper

1) Place the crumbled bacon and cooked shallot on top of the crust.
2) In a bowl, beat the eggs with the cream. Add the cheese, salt, and pepper. Be careful with the salt and pepper since the bacon/ham and the cheese are already salty.
3) Pour on top of the quiche dough.
4) Place in the oven for 40 to 45 minutes until golden. Remove from oven and let rest for 5 to 10 minutes.

Chicken Asparagus

- 2 cups cooked diced or shredded chicken (270 grams)
- ½ to 1 pound of blanched asparagus or broccoli, cooked 10 minutes then plunged in cold water (225 to 450 grams)
- 3 or 4 large eggs
- ¾ to 1 cup whipping cream
- 1 cup shredded Swiss or Gruyère cheese (110 grams)
- A dash of nutmeg
- Salt and pepper

1) Sprinkle the cooked and diced chicken on top of the quiche and arrange the asparagus or broccoli in a spoke fashion on top of the chicken.
2) In a bowl, beat the eggs, cream, and nutmeg. Add the shredded cheese. Add some salt and pepper, taking into consideration that the cheese is a little salty. Pour the mixture over the filling.
3) Place in the oven for 40 to 45 minutes until golden. Remove from oven and let rest for 5 to 10 minutes. It can be eaten warm or lukewarm. Serve with a salad for lunch or a light dinner.

Side Dishes

Glazed Carrots 140
Molded Rice 142
Au Gratin Potatoes 143
French Mac and Cheese 145
Mashed Potatoes 147
Summer Vegetable Stew 149

Glazed Carrots

Carottes glacées

My mom, Mamie Gisèle, used to make Carottes Vichy. The carrots were cooked in Vichy water and then drained. We added crème fraiche and sprinkled parsley. It was good but I did not like the boiled carrots.

I liked these better because they had a flavorful glaze. They were served as a side dish, at holiday meals, at Maxine Kopczynski's house and funnily enough, the recipe had this French title, so why not include this in my cookbook?

Serves 4 to 6   Intermediate

- 10/12 medium carrots cleaned, peeled, and cut into 2-inch cylinders or olive cut
- 1½ cup beef or chicken stock
- 4 tablespoons butter (57 grams)
- 2 tablespoons sugar (25 grams)
- ½ teaspoon salt
- Freshly ground pepper
- ¼ cup chopped parsley (6 grams)

Needed
- Paring knife
- Skillet
- Wooden spoon
- Heated serving dish

1) In an 8 to 10-inch skillet, bring the carrots, stock, butter, sugar, salt, and pepper to a boil on moderate heat. Cover and simmer over low heat, shaking the skillet occasionally so the carrots are coated with the liquid.

2) Check that the liquid is not cooking too fast. If it is, add more stock. Cook a few minutes still on low heat. The carrots should be tender when pierced with the tip of a sharp knife. The liquid should be a brown syrupy glaze.

3) If the stock has not reduced enough, remove the carrots to a plate and boil the liquid on high heat. Before serving, roll the carrots around in the pan to coat them with the glaze.

4) Transfer the carrots to a heated vegetable dish and sprinkle them with chopped parsley.

Molded Rice
Timbales de riz

I always use long grain rice when I am cooking French, however, to serve molded rice the short grain rice will stick together better.

Yields 4   Easy

- 1 tablespoon butter or margarine (14 grams)
- 1 cup short grain rice (160 grams)
- Thyme
- Salt and pepper
- 2 cups water or chicken broth

Needed

- 1 saucepan
- Glass or plastic cups about 6 ounces

1) Melt butter in a pan. Add the rice, thyme, salt, and pepper. When the rice has absorbed the fat, add the liquid, and cook until it is all absorbed, about 20 to 25 minutes.

2) Butter a 6 ounce plastic cup/glass and pack some rice tightly, pressing it down. Squeeze the sides to get the molded rice out and arrange around a platter with a dish that has sauce like a chicken with cream and olives.

Au Gratin Potatoes
Gratin dauphinois et gratin savoyard

Gratin dauphinois is often made of potatoes and cream without cheese, however, a lot of recipes include cheese in it.

The purists will tell you that if it has cheese, it is not a gratin dauphinois but indeed a gratin savoyard.

So, whatever it is, mine includes cheese because everything tastes better with cheese. It is always a classic at our house around the holidays as an accompaniment to white meats.

Serves 6 to 8   Easy

- 2 pounds potatoes, Yukon Gold works well (900 grams)
- 1 tablespoon butter (14 grams)
- 1 clove garlic
- 1½ cup whipping cream
- Salt and pepper
- 1 ½ cup shredded Gruyère cheese (170 grams)
- 1 egg

Needed
- Paring knife
- Large baking dish at least 9x13
- Small mixing bowl
- Small whisk

1) Preheat the oven to 400°F.

2) Peel the potatoes and slice them very thin. A mandolin works great.

3) Using a large baking dish, rub the butter and the clove of garlic on all the sides.

4) Spread one layer of potatoes, add salt and pepper, ¼ of the cream, and ¼ of the cheese.

5) Do a second layer of potatoes overlapping slightly like a tiled roof. Add the second quarter of the cream and then the cheese. Repeat process with third layer of potatoes. Add salt and pepper.

6) Top with the third quarter of the cream and the cheese.

7) Put in the oven and bake for 45 minutes to 1 hour.

8) 10 minutes before the end, beat 1 egg with the last quarter of the cream. Add salt and pepper. Pour on the top of the potatoes and sprinkle the leftover cheese. Add a few pieces of butter on the top.

9) Keep baking for another 10 minutes until the sauce thickens.

Tips

If you do not like the flavor of garlic, you could sprinkle a little grated nutmeg in the bottom of your dish for a different flavor.

When the gratin is almost done, the cream sometimes tends to separate or curdle. Mixing the beaten egg with the cream at the end, will remedy this problem and your sauce should look smoother.

French Mac and Cheese

Macaronis au gratin

This was a favorite at our house although growing up I was not too keen on eating pasta. Since I moved to the USA, my family here loves it. Mac & Cheese became an iconic American food when Thomas Jefferson's enslaved chef James Hemings brought the recipe to Virginia. When he served as Minister Plenipotentiary to the Court of Versailles between 1785-1789, Jefferson took Hemings with him to be trained in the culinary arts at the Château de Chantilly. When Hemings returned, he was fluent in French and had achieved the title of Chef de Cuisine. Hemings is also credited with being the first in America to make pommes frites—French Fries!

For the mornay sauce it is important to avoid lumps; this is accomplished by using a wire whisk or wooden spoon. Flour based sauces also require the use of a cold liquid to pour into the hot fat/flour mixture.

Serves 4 to 6   Intermediate

- ½ pound macaroni (225 grams)
- Salt and oil for water
- ¼ stick of butter (28 grams)
- 2 tablespoons flour (16 grams)
- Salt and pepper
- 2 cups cold milk or half and half
- A pinch of grated nutmeg
- 1 to 2 cups shredded Gruyère or Comté cheese (110 to 220 grams) depending on choice of breadcrumbs topping
- You can add 1 to 1½ cup breadcrumbs on top instead of the shredded cheese (optional)

Needed

- One large pot
- Colander
- Large saucepan
- Wooden spoon
- Whisk
- 9x13 baking dish or a round ceramic quiche dish – about 9½ inches in diameter

Macaroni

1) Boil 4 quarts water with salt and oil. Throw in the macaroni noodles in the boiling water and boil until tender and not too soft, al dente for about 8-10 minutes. For more tender, boil another minute. Drain well and prepare the mornay sauce.

2) Preheat the oven at 400°F.

Mornay sauce

1) On low heat, melt the butter in a saucepan. When it is sizzling, add the flour and cook a few seconds until foaming. Pour the cold milk or half and half gradually and keep stirring with a whisk until the mixture starts to thicken. Add salt and pepper and grated nutmeg.

2) When the sauce is ready, add half of the grated cheese keeping the other half to top dish unless using breadcrumb topping. Adjust the salt and pepper depending on how salty the cheese is.

3) Add the macaroni to the sauce.

4) Butter a baking dish and pour the macaroni mixture in it. Top with reserved cheese or breadcrumbs.

5) Bake for about 20 minutes until the cheese/breadcrumbs on top is golden brown and crispy.

Tips

You can double the quantities of the mornay for an even creamier sauce.

Mashed Potatoes
Purée de pommes de terre

Mamie Gisèle used to make purée on a regular basis. Being from Auvergne in the Massif Central of France, this was what the poor people ate because it was filling, so it was her go to side dish. The best part is when she cooked a meat with jus, not gravy, but a simple juice from the dregs of the shallots, tomato and ½ a glass of water or alcohol around the meat, that she would simmer covered after the meat was browned. Yum! Our daughter loved it when Mamie would serve the purée, then the meat and Mamie would ask her to make a well – un puits in the purée so the juice would not run on the plate. The trick was to eat the purée with the juice without any jus escaping on the plate!

Serves 4 to 6   Easy

- 3 pounds potatoes, Idaho, Russet, or Yukon gold (1300 grams)
- 1 stick salted butter, cold, cut in cubes (113 grams)
- ⅓ to ½ cup milk warmed
- Fresh ground pepper to taste

Needed

- Large pot
- Vegetable peeler or a paring knife
- Saucepan
- Strainer or colander
- Potato masher
- A wooden spoon

1) Peel and quarter the potatoes.

2) Cover in a pot with cold water bring to boil, reduce to simmer.

3) Cook for 20 or 25 minutes until tender when probed with knife.

4) Drain water and mash potatoes using a potato masher.

5) Add the cold salted cubed butter and the warm milk or half and half. Mix well.

6) Adjust seasoning with salt and add a generous amount of ground pepper.

7) You can add crushed garlic for extra flavor at the end (a favorite at our house).

8) Serve immediately.

Tips

Do not use a mixer or a food processor to make the *purée* because it will cause the mixture to become elastic and sticky.

Summer Vegetable Stew
Ratatouille

This is a popular dish from the south region of France, Provence. You can tell because it uses garlic, tomatoes, and olive oil, which are plentiful in this region close to Italy.

In the summer, there is nothing simpler than that vegetable stew that smells like sunshine. My mom, Mamie Gisèle, used to make this every summer. A favorite at our house!

Serves 4 to 6   Easy

- 2 to 3 medium cloves of garlic minced
- 2 medium yellow onions
- 2 average green peppers or other colorful peppers
- 2 small eggplants, Japanese eggplants work well
- 2 small zucchinis
- 1 pound juicy medium tomatoes, Roma preferred (450grams)
- 1 bouquet garni made from 1 bay leaf, 1 branch of thyme, 1 branch parsley tied with string to ease removal. Or use 1 teaspoon each of dried herbs.
- ½ cup olive oil
- Handful of basil
- 1 teaspoon Herbes de Provence
- Salt and pepper to taste

Needed
- Paring knife
- Large cooking pot

1) Cut the vegetables in 2-inch chunks, except for the onions and peppers that should be cut in strips and the garlic that will be minced.

2) Heat olive oil on medium or medium high. When shimmering add onions, garlic, and peppers. When soft add the other vegetables, the tomatoes being last, with the bouquet garni, salt, and pepper.

3) Cook for 1 to 1½ hours partially covered on medium heat. If there is too much liquid uncover halfway through to reduce. Mix while cooking on medium heat. Lower to simmer if the eggplant sticks to the pan.

4) Take off the heat. Let the ratatouille rest for 5 to 10 minutes before serving.

Tips

If you want a spicier dish, you can add ½ to 1 jalapeno pepper minced or any creole seasoning would be good. Piment d'Espelette, a French mild red pepper is a terrific addition, not as spicy as the jalapeno.

It tastes better reheated the next day. The flavors blend even better.

Ratatouille is usually eaten warm or hot as a side dish with a grilled or sautéed meat like pork chops or veal Osso Bucco. Tastes great with sauteed chicken thighs, or grilled salmon.

Cheese

Cheese in France 154
How to Properly Slice Cheese 156
Preparing a Cheese Tray 157

Cheese in France
Les fromages

Growing up in France you always finish a meal with a piece of cheese, some baguette, maybe a glass of red wine, and fruit. I remember when we used to go to my aunt and uncle's house in the Limousin region, we would eat the first and main course on a plate and when it was time for the cheese course, before dessert, we had to sop up our plate with bread well so we could turn it over and eat our cheese on the back of the plate.

In France, we have more than 400 different cheeses, not counting all the local ones. General Charles de Gaulle said once in the '60s, "How do you expect me to govern a country that has more than 360 different kinds of cheeses!" During the 2nd World War, Winston Churchill proclaimed: "Any country that has 300 cheeses cannot die!"

Fine cheese comes in a nearly infinite variety of flavors and textures. In France cheesemaking dates to the 13th century and was a civilization changing innovation that allowed, for the first time, a way to preserve surplus milk for later use. Cheese can be produced at home in a matter of hours or arrive at your table after a journey of between 3 and 36 months. Its rich and complex flavors come from its unique ingredients, the secrets and skills of the cheesemaker, and the transcendent combination of taste, smells, and textures coming from its rind (the drier and stronger flavored edge) and the heart of the cheese (the creamier and milder interior). Whatever the journey it has taken to your table you are the steward of the effort it took to make it and must do two things—serve it at a proper room temperature and know how to slice it in a manner so that every serving has the proper balance of rind and heart.

On this second point French people are very particular on how to slice cheeses and this is one of my pet peeves!! Depending on their shape, cheeses are sliced differently. If you want to have fun, stream the Arte video Karambolage on how to cut cheeses.

How to Slice Cheese Properly

Cheeses in France are cut based on their size and shapes. The golden rule is to make sure each person has an equal amount of rind and heart to avoid a family conflict!!

Cheeses that are small, round, and flat are cut in wedges like a cake, tart, or pizza. This includes cheeses such as Camembert, Reblochon, Neuchâtel, Epoisses, Fourme d'Ambert.

Large round, and flat cheeses like Brie are purchased whole or in triangular portions. You must cut long slices along the sides of the triangle (like the round cheeses in a small size) then you could cut that piece in half if it is too big. Other option: You could cut portions across the width from the point on the diagonal and when you get to the rind, cut long pieces from the rind to the heart.

Pyramids and cylinders like Valençay et Charollais are cut in wedges in the same manner as small round cheeses like a cake or pizza from the top to the bottom in triangles.

Munster, Maroilles, Livarot and other square cheeses are cut diagonally so you end up with two triangles. Each triangle is cut in half and halved again until you get the desired portion size. (4, 8, 16 equal parts).

Logs of cheese like Chèvre (goat cheese), Sainte-Maure de Touraine are sliced in parallel slices after removing the ends. With the Sainte-Maure de Touraine, remove the straw first before slicing!

Wedges of wheels of Comté, Gruyère, Morbier, Jarlsberg, and a few blue cheeses are sliced parallel to the rind and about halfway there, cut rectangular pieces from the rind to the heart or cut in a fan shape.

Blue cheeses such as Roquefort, Fourme d'Ambert, Bleu d'Auvergne, Gorgonzola, Cambozola have the strongest flavors concentrated in the blue veined parts of the cheese, so it is important not to wrong any guest at the table. Blue cheeses sold in quarters like Roquefort, must be served on the flat side and cut in a fan shape so everyone gets the rind and the heart. Blue cheeses in cylinder form, like the Fourme d'Ambert, are sold in big slices and would be cut like a round cheese (see above).

For runny cheeses, say a Mont d'Or remove the rind delicately and serve the cheese with a tablespoon.

Very hard cheeses like extra old Mimolette, Tête de Moine can be shaved with a vegetable peeler or broken off in pieces. For the Tête de Moine, it is cut in flowers with a *girolle*, a special tool found at cheese shops.

Preparing a Cheese Tray

A broad selection for a *plateau de fromages* would be to 4 or 5 different cheeses:

- One hard cheese like a Comté or a Gruyère,
- One soft cheese like a Brie or Camembert,
- One blue cheese like a Roquefort, Bleu d'Auvergne, Gorgonzola or Cambozola,
- One goat cheese, fresh or hard,
- One sheep's milk cheese like a Manchego, Osso Iraty, or Petit Basque.

Remember cheese needs to be at room temperature to appreciate the full flavor. Take it out of the fridge at least 1 hour before serving.

If you serve a variety of cheeses on a platter put out several knives so you do not mix the flavors between them.

Desserts

Rum Baba 160

Flambéed Bananas 163

Crème Caramel 165

Dessert Crepes 168

How to Fold a Crepe 172

Swan Cream Puffs 175

Mont Blanc Dessert 178

Financiers 180

Clafoutis 183

Rum Chocolate Cake 185

Yogurt Cake 189

Floating Island and Snow Eggs 191

Lemon Madeleines 195

Chocolate Mousse 198

Nougat Ice Cream 200

Grand Marnier Soufflé 203

Apricot Tart 206

Apple Tart or Apple Galette 208

Strawberry Tart 211

Raspberry Tartlets 215

Almond Tuiles 219

Rum Baba

Baba au Rhum

Baba au Rhum is called Babka in Polish. This recipe is attributed to Stanislaw Leszczynski, King of Poland, exiled to Lorraine, who became Duke of Lorraine in the 18th century.

It was a dry Kugelhopf dipped in rum. Nicolas Stohrer is the pastry chef who created a recipe to make the dry Kugelhopf moist and more delicous.

My dad's recipe used yeast, but I found it easier and faster to use baking powder.

Serves 8 to 10   Intermediate

- ½ cup sugar (100 grams)
- 3 large eggs separated
- 3 tablespoons milk
- 1 cup flour (120 grams)
- 2 tablespoons of baking powder (28 grams)
- ½ stick of butter at room temperature (55 grams)

- One pinch salt for the egg whites
- Candied fruit or fresh fruit like strawberries/raspberries for garnish
- 1 to 1½ cups whipped cream flavored with 1 teaspoon rum, kirsch, or vanilla (120 to 180 grams)

For the syrup

- ⅔ cup granulated sugar (130 grams)
- 1⅓ cups water
- ¼ cup rum or kirsch

For the glaze

- 1 to 2 tablespoons apricot jam dissolved in ½ that quantity of water, rum or kirsch.

Needed

- 2 mixing bowls or the ones attached to the stand mixer
- 1 small saucepan
- Spatula
- A baba mold or a Bundt pan
- A deep serving dish
- A pastry brush
- 1 small saucepan

1) Preheat the oven to 375°F.
2) Butter and flour a baba mold that looks like a doughnut mold, or a Bundt pan that holds about 6 to 8 cups.
3) Combine flour and baking powder by sifting and set aside.
4) Beat the egg yolks with the sugar in a stand mixer, using the paddle attachment, until the mixture becomes thick and pale yellow in color.
5) Gradually add the milk to egg mixture on slow speed.

6) Remove from mixer and slowly fold in dry ingredients. Add the ½ stick of softened butter.

7) In a dry and clean bowl, beat the egg whites with a pinch of salt, using the whisk attachment of the stand mixer. Make sure the egg whites are beaten to the stiff peak stage. You should be able to turn the bowl upside down over your head without any fear of the egg whites dripping on you!

8) Incorporate ⅓ of the whites at a time, to the egg yolk mixture, folding them in delicately with a spatula. The egg yolk mixture will be dense so fold, do not beat. Make sure all the whites are incorporated.

9) Spread an even layer of the mixture in the mold. It should be about ⅓ filled.

10) Bake for 20 minutes.

11) During the baking time, prepare the syrup. Boil the sugar and water. Off the heat, add the rum, or kirsch.

12) When the baba is baked, take it out of the oven and unmold it right away on a deep serving dish. Pour the warm syrup everywhere on the baba, making sure you are not leaving any part of the baba dry. You can poke it with a toothpick in different areas to make sure the hot syrup gets everywhere.

13) Mix the apricot jam with water or a spirit of your choice. Heat it up a little bit in a saucepan and brush the baba with a pastry brush to give it that professional look.

14) Decorate with candied fruit or seasonal fruit like strawberries or raspberries. The hole in the middle is usually filled with whipped cream flavored with rum, kirsch, or vanilla.

Flambéed Bananas
Bananes flambées

This is a favorite of my husband Jean. When bananas are over ripened, we do not make banana bread, we make bananes flambées! We use any kind of liquor that we have to flambé them. You can slice the bananas any way you would like.

Serves 4   Intermediate

- 1 to 2 tablespoons of butter
- 3 to 4 bananas peeled, cut in half and then lengthwise
- 1 tablespoon of brown sugar
- 1 tablespoon of Grand Marnier, Cognac, rum, or other liquor with at least 40% alcohol

Needed
- ➢ Paring knife
- ➢ Frying pan
- ➢ Matches or lighter

1) In a frying pan, melt butter on medium heat. When it is sizzling, add the cut bananas and sprinkle with the sugar.

2) When they start to caramelize, pour the alcohol and when warm, light a match and bring it close to the dish so it lights up. Swirl the pan around to burn all the alcohol.

3) Serve as is or with whipped cream or vanilla ice-cream!

Tips

Do not use the kitchen fan when you flambé.

Crème Caramel

Crème renversée au caramel

My mom, who did not like to make most desserts, liked to make this one. She used to call it oeufs au lait – eggs with milk. The funny story is that once it was put in the ramequins, she was too nervous to unmold it on a plate and my dad was dying to turn it over to watch the caramel drizzle down on his plate! So, she finally decided to buy some ready-made commercial crème caramel that my dad could flip over on his plate, to his heart content, and everybody was happy!! We all have fond memories of it!

In my recipe I use a ⅓ cup sugar for the custard because we do not like it too sweet, but you can put up to ⅔ cup or more if you want! Be creative.

Serves 4 to 6   Advanced

- ⅓ to ⅔ cup granulated sugar (67-130 grams)
- 3 cups of whole milk
- 1 teaspoon vanilla
- 4 large eggs

For the caramel

- ½ cup granulated sugar (100 grams)
- A few drops of lemon juice
- 3 tablespoons water

Needed

- 4 to 6 cup oven proof soufflé dish, a non-stick metal mold or 4 10-ounce oven proof ramequins
- 1 small saucepan
- 1 medium saucepan
- Whisk
- Hot water for water bath
- Large ovenproof baking dish

1) Preheat oven to 400°F.
2) In a saucepan put the sugar, the drops of lemon and the water. Cook on medium heat. Swirl the pan around to dissolve the sugar. Do not stir. When the sugar is dissolved, boil for several minutes. When the bubbles become thick, swirl around the mixture. When the edges become brown, remove it from the heat. It will continue to darken as you swirl the pan around.
3) Pour the caramel into the soufflé dishes, quickly roll it around to coat the bottom and on the kitchen counter to coat the sides. If using individual molds pour about a tablespoon of caramel per mold.
4) Boil some water.
5) In a different saucepan scald milk -- bring to just below boiling 180°F.
6) In a bowl combine the eggs, sugar, and vanilla and beat slowly with a fork. You should not create foam. Gradually pour the scalded milk on the eggs while stirring with a whisk by hand to temper the eggs. It should thicken a little.
7) Place the caramelized mold(s) in the large oven proof baking dish and fill with thickened egg mixture up to about ¼ inch from the top. Pour the hot water into the oven proof baking dish to make a water bath. The water

should be about 1½ inches high if using a 4 to 6 cup soufflé dish, and about ½ inch if using individual ramequins.

8) Place the water filled baking dish with the mold(s) in it, in the oven and bake for 30 to 45 minutes if using a single soufflé dish. Reduce time to 25 to 30 minutes for ramequins. It should not boil. The cream is ready when firm to the touch and covered with a golden crust.

9) Let cool completely, about 30 minutes before unmolding. You can refrigerate at this point. When cold, you can run a knife along the edge and turn the mold(s) over on an inverted plate and serve.

Tips

The lemon juice will prevent the sugar from crystallizing and will keep the caramel liquid.

If you have some caramel left at the bottom of the saucepan or the mold, you can add 3 tablespoons of hot water. It will stop the caramelization, and it will also stay liquid. Bring back to a boil on the heat, scraping the bottom with a wooden spoon. Pour the leftover caramel sauce over the unmolded crème caramel.

If you want to skip the caramel portion, you can make eggs in milk as my mom, Mamie Gisèle, used to make it. Serve in individual ramequins so it can be eaten without unmolding.

Dessert Crepes

Crêpes sucrées

The French are famous for Crêpes Suzette, which are crepes in an orange sauce, with the juice and zest of two oranges, flambéed in Cointreau or Grand Marnier. In Normandy, the crepes are served stuffed with sliced sautéed apples and flambéed in Calvados—Apple Jack. They can also be filled with strawberries topped with whipped cream and are delicious with pastry cream. My favorite is filled with orange marmalade and sprinkled with Grand Marnier. You can flambé crepes with dark rum, brandy or Cognac, Cointreau or Grand Marnier that has been warmed.

All these fillings are for crepes that you have made in advance.

Yields about 16 crepes   Intermediate

For crepes

- 4 large eggs
- 2 cups all-purpose white flour (250 grams)
- ½ teaspoon salt
- 2½ cups whole or 2% milk

- 3 tablespoons melted butter (43 grams)
- 1 tablespoon sugar (13 grams)
- 2 teaspoons vanilla

Needed

- Stand or handheld mixer
- 8-inch non-stick frying pan or a de Buyer metal crepe pan
- Ladle
- Pastry brush
- Spatula
- Plate
- Small frying pan
- Soup spoon
- Lighter or matches

1) Mix the eggs first then slowly add the flour and salt. Gradually add the milk to help the flour be less sticky and at the end, when the mixture is smooth, add the melted butter, sugar, and vanilla.

2) You can leave it at room temperature for all the ingredients to blend. Usually, the batter thickens a little. If it is too thick, add a little milk so the batter is more fluid.

3) A small nonstick pan is perfect for the job. Use a brush to oil the pan lightly. You can use margarine, or oil but not olive oil. Use medium high heat.

4) When the pan is hot, and the oil is shimmering throw a little cold water on the oil to see if it sizzles. Take it off the heat and pour about ¼ to ⅓ cup of batter slowly, start first with half of that, on the pan as you are swirling it quickly, so it spreads very thin. You might not use the whole quantity. If there is not enough spreading on the pan, you can add a little more in the bare spots. After a while you will know what quantity to use in the pan you have.

5) Cook until bubbles form and when the edges become brown run a spatula

to detach the sides of the crepe. Flip it over with your fingers and a spatula. Cook the other side for a shorter time, 1 minute at the most. The crepe is ready when the center is soft, and the edges are crispy.

6) Stack on a plate and keep warm in a 150°F oven covered with foil.

Crepes Suzette

- 2 squeezed oranges
- ½ stick of butter (56 grams)
- 4 to 5 tablespoons white sugar (50 to 63 grams)
- 1 tablespoon Grand Marnier, Cointreau, Triple Sec or Drambuie or any orange flavored liqueur
- ¾ to 1 ounce brandy (optional)

1) Melt the butter with the orange juice. Add the sugar and bring to a boil. Pour a little liqueur. Warm up the already made crepes in the pan juices and baste them with a spoon. Crepes will be served folded in 4. You can flambé them at the end at the table with ¾ to 1 ounce of hot brandy.

Normandy Style Crepes

- 4 Golden Delicious apples about 1 pound (450 grams)
- ½ stick of butter (56 grams)
- 3 tablespoons sugar white or brown (36 grams)
- ¼ cup rum or Apple Jack – Calvados (optional)
- Raisins and cinnamon if you like

1) Cook the sliced apples in the butter for 10 minutes. When cooked sprinkle with sugar so the apples can caramelize, taking a slightly brown color.

2) You can wet the apples with rum or Calvados/Apple Jack and flambé now or wait till they are stuffed in the already made crepes and flambé then.

3) Upon serving, sprinkle the crepes with confectioner's sugar.

You can substitute the apples with bananas, pineapple, and shredded coconut for a Hawaiian flair!

Jam Filled Crepes

You can make these crepes as you go, they are better if you eat them right after you made them.

I recommend plain crepes sprinkled with sugar and any flavored liqueur. The best jams for that are: strawberry, orange marmalade, red currant jelly and apricot jam.

The crepes can be layered with jam and stacked up then cut in wedges like a cake.

How to Fold a Crepe

Crepes can be used to form a variety of shapes depending on how you wish to serve them and the chosen fillings.

Traditional, fold two opposing sides to meet in the middle

Quartered, fold in half and half again

Rolled

Pocket, fold opposing sides to overlap in the middle, fold bottom up ⅔ of the way

Stacked and layered with a filling, like a cake

Open middle, four sides folded inward leaving the center open for filling

Swan Cream Puffs

Cygnes de Montjeu

These cream puffs were the specialty of a pastry shop I worked at as a teenager in my hometown of Autun, in Burgundy. They were called Cygnes de Montjeu, Swans of Montjeu, named after an estate and a château outside the city. Every time the swans had a broken neck, the pastry chef would not consider them acceptable to be sold, so he would send them home with me, for my family to enjoy!! What a delight!!

They are even more elegant than the usual cream puffs. These are made in pastry shops and are not country cooking or family cooking, but it is nice to be fancy sometimes!! They make a statement at the end of a dinner and are not any more difficult than regular cream puffs. So, go for it! Try them!!

With this choux pastry you can also make eclairs, croquembouches, chouquettes and other desserts like Paris-Brest, Saint-Honoré, and accompaniments like Pommes Dauphines.

Makes 8 to 10 swans   Advanced

Choux pastry

- 1 cup water
- 1 stick unsalted butter (113 grams)
- 1½ tablespoon granulated sugar (18 grams)

- 1 cup all-purpose flour (120 grams)
- 4 large eggs

Needed

- 1 medium saucepan
- Stand or handheld mixer
- Mixing bowl
- 1 or 2 greased cookie sheets
- Pastry bag with tip or a Ziploc plastic bag with a bottom corner slightly cut

1) Preheat the oven to 425°F.
2) On medium heat, boil the water, butter, and sugar in a saucepan.
3) When it boils, take it off the heat and pour in the whole cup of flour. Mix vigorously with a wooden spoon until all the flour is absorbed.
4) Put the dough back on the heat to dry it up. Keep mixing until the dough comes off the sides of the pan and makes a ball. It should also leave a film at the bottom of the pan. This is a key step to help dry the dough.
5) Off the heat, add one egg at a time and mix well after each addition. You can use a mixer at this point. The dough must be smooth.
6) You can put the dough in the fridge for 30 minutes so the choux will puff up more when baked.
7) Use a small tip for the pastry bag and fill it in with ¼ of the dough to make the swan's necks. To allow for breakage pipe 10 to 12 necks in a S shape on a greased cookie sheet.
8) On a separate prepared baking sheet make the swans' bodies by forming 1x1½ inch oval heaps of dough with a pastry bag with large tip or a tablespoon. Make 9 to 10 ovals spaced 2 inches apart.
9) Bake the necks for 10 minutes until slightly golden. Bake the bodies 20 to 25 minutes until slightly golden.
10) Turn off the oven and leave the door ajar to dry for 5 minutes before re-

moving. This is a key step to avoid collapsing of the choux pastry.

11) Cool on a rack before filling the bodies with whipped cream.

Tips

Check your oven temperature with an oven thermometer. Use it as your guide to achieve the correct baking temperature for a specific recipe.

These must be made the day of. Making them in the morning and having the whipped cream ready in the fridge will free time for last minute assembly.

Whipped cream

- 4 cups heavy whipping cream
- 3 tablespoons granulated sugar (38 grams)
- 1 tablespoon of pure vanilla or almond extract

Needed

➢ Cold beaters from a mixer and cold bowl

1) Make sure to put the beaters and bowl in the fridge that are going to be used to whip the cream. It will be easier to whip this way.
2) When the cream is whipped add the sugar and flavoring.

How to assemble the swans at the last minute

1) Cut horizontally the top third of the bodies. Place the top thirds aside.
2) Fill the bottom ⅔ with whipped cream.
3) Place the necks in the cream.
4) Cut top thirds in half lengthwise to make the wings. Place the wings in the cream on each side. If you want a little tail, you can use a lemon zest! Serve immediately.

Mont Blanc Dessert

Dessert Mont-Blanc

This dessert is made with chestnut spread, Faugier if possible. This was a classic at our house because it was easy to make and in France you always had chestnut spread on hand for winter and the holidays. You can buy it online in the USA.

This is my most favorite flavor. In France they have chestnut jam, chestnut ice cream, and candied chestnuts called marrons glacés that we eat around the holidays.

It is called Mont Blanc because it is named after the highest mountain in France. The whipped cream reminds us of its white peak.

Serves 6   Easy

- 1 can of chestnut spread (500 grams)
- 1 large or several small vanilla meringue cookies broken up
- 8 ounces whipped cream with 2 tablespoon sugar and 1 teaspoon vanilla
- 6 marrons glacés — candied chestnuts (optional)
- 3 ounces dark semi-sweet chocolate (85 grams)

Needed

- ➢ Stand or handheld mixer
- ➢ Medium mixing bowl
- ➢ Paring knife or vegetable peeler
- ➢ 6 parfait glasses

1) Beat the whipping cream with sugar and vanilla. Refrigerate.

2) Break chocolate into small pieces or shave it for decoration.

3) Break up the meringue cookies in small pieces.

4) In 6 individual parfait glasses layer the chestnut spread, meringue, chocolate pieces, and the marrons glacés.

5) Place some whipped cream on top of the chestnut/meringue mixture in the glass bowls.

6) Add a few pieces of chocolate to decorate.

7) Refrigerate until ready to serve.

Financiers

Financiers

These are small almond cakes, which are a favorite of mine, moist inside and crispy on the outside. They are made in small rectangular molds with slightly flared sides which resemble a gold bar or ingot.

It became popular in the Paris financial district of La Bourse — the French stock exchange, in the 19th century. It was created at the Pâtisserie Lasne next to the Bourse. The hurried brokers would buy it for a quick snack, as fast food that they could eat on the run without needing a fork or knife. Without frosting or powdered sugar, it was not messy and would hold up in someone's pocket or satchel without being crushed.

They are usually eaten for a morning or midafternoon snack. Great with a cup of coffee or tea.

Serves 6   Easy

- ¾ cup powdered sugar (100 grams)
- 2½ tablespoons flour (20 grams)
- 7 tablespoons almond flour (50 grams)

- 2 egg whites
- ½ teaspoon vanilla (optional)
- 4 tablespoons unsalted butter (60 grams)
- 1 tablespoon sliced almonds (10 grams)
- Butter and flour for the mold

Neededs

- Sifter or Sieve
- 2 bowls
- Fork
- Saucepan
- Mold for 6 financiers or muffin mold

1) Preheat the oven to 400°F. Butter and flour the mold.
2) Mix the sugar, flours, and sift into a bowl.
3) Mix the egg whites slightly with a fork and combine with sifted ingredients.
4) In a light-colored saucepan use the butter to make brown butter, *beurre noisette*. Cut the butter into smaller pieces so it melts evenly. Continue to heat through the sputtering stage as the water is boiled off. Continue to stir and monitor closely as butter starts to turn golden and brown. Dark brown milk solids will form on the bottom of the pan, and you should notice a pleasant nutty caramel aroma. When you have achieved the desired level of browning transfer to a heat proof bowl off stove to halt cooking. Add to the previous mixture and mix well.
5) Distribute the dough among the 6 financiers. Sprinkle with sliced almonds
6) Place the mold in the oven and bake for 18-20 minutes. Time will vary depending on the size of your mold. It should be dark gold before you take it out.

7) Let cool before unmolding.

Tips

You can make the batter the day before and refrigerate it. The next day bake it.

If you do not have a financier mold you can use a muffin mold.

One or two blueberries or raspberries may be substituted for the sliced almonds.

This is a good and quick way to use your egg whites if you do not want to make meringues or macarons!

You can serve them with hot chocolate, a lemon cream or by themselves.

Clafoutis

Flauniarde (Flognarde) ou Clafoutis

This is a family dessert. My mom, who did not make most desserts, would make this one because she could make it in her sleep! It is a crepe batter. It originates from where she grew up in the Auvergne and Limousin area.

Flognarde is a dessert with apples or pears. Clafoutis is a dessert with cherries. They are both versions of the same quick dessert that was served in the countryside in the Limousin and Auvergne regions of France where my family is from. It can be made in a square, rectangular, round pan. It does not matter!

At the end of the day during hay season the farmers used to share this dessert, served right off the baking mold. No plate was passed to limit the dishwashing and to add to the conviviality. When using cherries, the pits were left because they are supposed to give an almond flavor to the clafoutis! Then you can have a pit spitting contest afterwards!

Serves 4 to 8   Easy

- 4 large eggs
- ⅔ cup granulated sugar (130 grams)
- A pinch of salt
- ⅔ cup all-purpose flour (83 grams)
- 1 cup of milk
- 4 tablespoons of melted butter (57 grams)
- 1 teaspoon of kirsch or vanilla for flavoring
- 1 pound apples, pears, apricots, peaches, plums, prunes, berries, or cherries (450 grams)

Needed

- Stand mixer or handheld mixer
- 1 large mixing bowl
- Square or round glass or ceramic 8 to 9-inch mold, buttered

1) Preheat your oven to 400°F.
2) Butter an 8 to 9-inch square or circular ceramic or glass mold. Slice the apples or pears. Cut the peaches, plums, or apricots in half and remove the pits. For cherries and prunes, remove the stems and pits. Dry the fruit if they have been washed. Place the fruit at the bottom of the mold in any fashion you want. Be creative!
3) In a mixer beat the eggs, sugar, and salt. The more you beat them, the more the batter will puff up while baking.
4) Gradually add the flour so you do not get lumps and mix well. The batter should be smooth.
5) Add the milk gradually and then the cooled butter. Mix until the batter is the consistency of a crepe batter. Add the flavoring.
6) Pour the batter over the fruit and bake for 45 minutes.
7) The dessert will puff up on the edges. It will come down if left out of the oven for too long.
8) Before serving, sprinkle the top with confectioner's sugar.

Tips

You can eat it hot or lukewarm, plain or with ice cream or whipped cream.

Rum Chocolate Cake
Gâteau au chocolat au rhum

When I found my dad's recipe cards, he had so many versions of gâteau au chocolat with different amount of sugar, chocolate, eggs, cream, it was mind boggling!

I have always liked chocolate cake with little or no flour. Such cakes are so moist and rich in flavor, the fact they often sink in the middle does not worry me at all. It is a fault remedied by turning it upside down before glazing. I have tasted Reine de Saba, Queen of Sheba cake as a child in France, Sacher Torte in Austria, so this is my own version!

Serves 8 to 10   Advanced

For the cake

- 6 ounces of bittersweet or semi-sweet baking chocolate (170 grams)
- 1 stick unsalted butter cut up in pieces (113 grams)
- 4 large room temperature eggs separated
- ½ cup granulated sugar (100 grams)
- 1 cup coarsely ground hazelnuts/filberts (110 grams)

- ¼ cup rum

For the glaze

- 3 ounces of bittersweet or semisweet baking chocolate (85 grams)
- 3 tablespoons unsalted butter (43 grams)
- Apricot jam (optional)

For chocolate leaves

- 1 ounce of chocolate of your choice: dark, milk or white for contrast (28 grams)
- A few camelia, holly, rose or ivy leaves washed and dried

Needed

- Double boiler
- Wooden spoon
- 9-inch round cake pan
- Parchment paper
- Stand or handheld mixer
- 2 large mixing bowls
- Cake rack
- Candy thermometer

Prepare the cake

1) Preheat the oven to 375°F.

2) Melt the chocolate and the butter in a double boiler until almost melted. Do not overheat. When almost melted, take off the heat and stir the chocolate with a wooden spoon until smooth. Let it cool and set aside. You could melt the chocolate in a microwave oven in 30 seconds increments.

3) Butter a 9-inch round cake pan and place a circle of parchment paper on the bottom.

4) Beat the egg yolks with the sugar until they are pale lemon color, and they have a thick consistency.

5) Add the cooled chocolate gradually, the ground up nuts, then the rum.

6) In another clean and dry large bowl, beat the egg whites with a pinch of salt. Beat until stiff peaks form. You should be able to turn the bowl upside down over your head without getting wet.

7) With a spatula, fold in ⅓ of the whites into the chocolate mixture and gradually add the rest of the whites by thirds.

8) Pour into the baking pan and bake for 25 minutes.

9) The center should still be soft. Cool in the pan 10 minutes. Unmold and place on a cake rack. Remove the parchment paper and cool for 20 minutes.

Prepare the glaze

1) Melt the chocolate at a temperature not higher than 120°F on the candy thermometer, then cool until spreading consistency, between 80 and 120°F.

2) You can spread a layer of apricot jam under the glaze much as they do for the Sacher Torte in Vienna.

3) Spread the glaze on the top and the sides of the cake once the chocolate is cooled. The chocolate should not be too runny but a good spreading consistency like honey.

Make chocolate leaves

1) Melt the chocolate in a double boiler or in the microwave in 30 second increments. Cool until spreading consistency is reached when the temperature of the chocolate is between 80 and 120°F.

2) Take a leaf that will be strong enough and will not tear. Spread the chocolate evenly on the underside of the leaf, making sure it does not run on the top side of the leaf.

3) Put the leaves in the freezer for 5 or 10 minutes.

4) When the chocolate is hardened, pull the leaf away from the chocolate, making sure not to leave any finger marks on the top of the chocolate leaf.

5) Place on the cake immediately or keep in a covered box in the freezer.

You can decorate this cake as pictured using broken flat chocolate pieces.

Needed

- Cookie sheet
- Metal spatula
- Parchment paper
- Chef's knife

1) Melt 1 to 2 ounces (28 to 56 grams) of chocolate of your choice in a double boiler: dark, milk or white for contrast.

2) When spreading consistency, spread the chocolate with a spatula, on a cookie sheet covered with parchment paper. Put in the freezer for an hour.

3) When the chocolate hardened, break up the sheet of chocolate in uneven pieces with the heel of a chef's knife.

4) Make sure to touch the chocolate pieces only on the underside not leaving any finger marks on the top.

5) Place a few of the flat broken pieces on top of the cake here and there in a free form. Sprinkle with powdered sugar.

Tips

This cake can be served plain and is also good served with whipped cream or the raspberry coulis recipe on page 202. This cake can be baked into 2, 8-inch round cake pans. In that case reduce the baking to just 10 to 15 minutes. Between the two layers you could spread apricot jam, raspberry jam, or whipped cream.

Yogurt Cake

Gâteau au yaourt

My mom would let us make this because it was foolproof and not messy to make. We used to eat it with jam, or honey after we came home from school for our goûter.

Here is my dad's recipe from his cousin Marie-Louise Martinie, from Le Pont du Mas in the Corrèze area, in the Limousin region of southwest France. She lived to 102. They had beehives in the Monédières mountains and made raw honey.

Serves 8 to 10   Easy

- One small 6 to 8 ounce plain yogurt (180-227 grams) save the container it will be your measuring cup
- 2 large eggs
- 3 yogurt containers of flour
- 2 teaspoons baking powder
- ½ container of safflower oil
- 1½ container of granulated sugar
- 1 teaspoon vanilla
- 1 teaspoon rum
- Powdered sugar

Needed

- ➢ Large mixing bowl
- ➢ The yogurt container as a measuring cup
- ➢ 8-inch square, round, or a quick bread pan

➢ Serving plate

1) Preheat the oven to 375°F.
2) Empty the yogurt in a big bowl.
3) Mix the 2 eggs in the bowl with the yogurt
4) Gradually add the flour with the baking powder. Beat well making sure there are no lumps.
5) Add the oil.
6) Add the sugar and beat well making sure there are no lumps.
7) Add the vanilla and the rum. Mix well.
8) Place in a buttered round, square or a quick bread cake pan.
9) Bake for 30 to 40 minutes. Test with toothpick for doneness.
10) Let the cake cool on a rack. Unmold on a serving plate, when cooled.
11) Before serving, sprinkle powdered sugar on top.

Floating Island and Snow Eggs
Ile flottante et Oeufs à la neige

My mom, Mamie Gisèle, used to make this by poaching the egg whites in water or in milk. It was a quick dessert served with a crème anglaise.

In this version the egg whites are baked in a water bath. I like this recipe better because it is easier to determine when the egg whites are done. This recipe is finished with a drizzle of caramel over the meringue, another bonus in my book!

You can make the crème anglaise and toast the almonds ahead of time. You bake the meringue in the early afternoon of your dinner and make the caramel at the last minute when you assemble the dish with meringue, cream, caramel and toasted sliced almonds.

Serves 4 to 6   Advanced

For the meringue

- 4 large egg whites at room temperature
- A pinch salt
- ¼ teaspoon cream of tartar

- ½ cup granulated sugar (100 grams)
- ¼ cup toasted sliced almonds for garnish (optional)

For the crème anglaise

- 1 cup half and half or whipping cream
- 4 large egg yolks
- 6 tablespoons granulated sugar (75 grams)
- 1 teaspoon vanilla

For the caramel

- ½ cup sugar (100 grams)

Needed

- Stand mixer with the egg white beater attachment
- Two mixing bowls
- 4 to 6 cup baking dish or 4 8 to 10-ounce ramequins buttered and sprinkled with powdered sugar.
- 9x13 baking dish
- 2 saucepans with a heavy bottom
- Wooden spoon
- Sieve or strainer
- Parchment paper
- Deep serving dish or individual serving bowls

For the meringue

1) Preheat the oven to 325°F.
2) Prepare baking dish by buttering sides and bottom, coat with sugar.
3) In a mixer beat egg whites until foaming. Add a pinch of salt and continue beating until soft peaks form. Add the cream of tartar continue beating

until stiff peaks form. Add sugar beating until incorporated and peaks become shiny.

4) Boil water for the water bath.

5) Pour the mixture into prepared baking dish. You could use individual ramequins, but you will need to adjust the baking time. The molds should be ⅔ to ¾ full to allow the meringue to rise during baking. Place the 4 to 6 cup baking dish in the 9x13 water bath and add about 1½ inches boiling water. If using individual ramequins, pour about ½ inch high of boiling water.

6) Bake for about 15-20 minutes. The meringue should rise a few inches and be slightly golden on top. Test with a cake tester to make sure it comes out clean.

7) When done remove from water bath and set aside to cool.

For the crème anglaise

1) While the meringue is baking scald the milk in a saucepan.

2) In a stand mixer, beat the egg yolks while adding the sugar gradually. The mixture should be thicker and pale yellow in color.

3) Blend ⅓ of the hot milk gradually into the yolk mixture to temper. As the yolks are slowly warming up, pour in the rest of the hot milk and mix well.

4) Return the crème anglaise to stove on low heat. Do not overheat or you will end up with scrambled eggs. Keep stirring with a wooden spoon as it thickens slowly.

5) The crème is ready when you can run your finger on the back of the spoon, and it leaves a clean trace. Add the vanilla off the heat. Strain the cream in a sieve to make sure you have no lumps.

For the caramel

1) In a saucepan put the sugar. Cook on medium heat.

2) As smoke comes up and the sides are getting brown, mix with a wooden spoon or fork, it will turn to caramel but will be lumpy! Keep stirring until

all the crystals are dissolved.

3) Remove from heat. Keep stirring. It will continue to darken.

4) With a tablespoon or fork drizzle strands of caramel on parchment paper for practice. When satisfied with the result drizzle the remainder of the caramel on top of the meringue.

To serve

1) Pour the crème anglaise in a deep serving dish or individual bowls. Run a knife around the meringue dish and flip it over on a separate plate. You can either slide the whole meringue on top of the crème anglaise or cut it into 4 or 6 pieces and float like icebergs on the crème anglaise. You can also place the meringue in a deep dish and pour the crème anglaise around it.

2) Drizzle with caramel and sprinkle toasted sliced almonds on top for garnish.

Tips

The crème anglaise can be served warm, lukewarm, or cold, in which case it can be made ahead of time and kept in the fridge for several days

Lemon Madeleines
Madeleines au citron

There are different versions about the origins of the madeleine, but it seems to have appeared in the 1700's around the town of Commercy in the Lorraine region of northeast France. A young girl, named Madeleine, baked them for Stanislaus Leszczynski, King of Poland, and Duke of Lorraine, according to her grandmother's recipe. Louis XV served them to his wife, Marie Leszczynska, daughter of Stanislaus, after a trip to Lorraine, then, she introduced them to the French court of Versailles.

In 1913, Marcel Proust wrote about eating a madeleine dipped in tea and memories from his childhood came flooding back. We all have our "madeleine de Proust" when you smell or taste something in the present and emotional memories from the past come to life again. This has become a key part of French culture.

I have tried many recipes for madeleine, and this is the one that puffs up the most. This is a recipe from my aunt Marie Martinie Verliat, who was married to a baker from Corrèze, a medieval town in the Limousin region, southwest France. I added lemon to her recipe for extra flavor.

Yields about 20   Intermediate

- 4 large eggs

- ⅔ cup granulated sugar (134 grams)
- 1½ stick cut up butter melted then cooled for no more than 20 minutes (170 grams)
- ¾ teaspoon pure vanilla
- 1 teaspoon lemon zest grated (just the yellow zest)
- 1½ cup all-purpose flour (192 grams)
- 1½ tablespoon baking powder (20 grams)

Needed

- ➢ Stand mixer
- ➢ Microwavable small bowl
- ➢ Spatula
- ➢ Madeleine mold preferably non stick

1) Preheat the oven to 400°F.
2) Melt the cut-up butter by 30 seconds increments in the microwave and let cool.
3) Beat the eggs and the sugar until pale yellow and thick. It should be double the volume and fluffy. A stand mixer works great!
4) Pour the cooled melted butter over the mixture.
5) Add the vanilla and the lemon zest.
6) Take the bowl off the stand mixer. In a sieve, put the flour and baking powder and sprinkle the mixture over the egg/sugar mixture, folding the flour/baking powder gradually with a spatula, until it is completely mixed.
7) Grease your metal mold with a spray.
8) Fill in your madeleine mold only ⅔ full and place in the middle of the oven.
9) Bake for about 10 minutes depending how much you filled your mold.

10) Let your madeleines rest for 10 minutes before unmolding.

Tips

If you want your madeleines to puff up more, you can put the batter in the fridge for 2 hours either in a bowl or in the madeleine mold. If you use a metal mold, they will puff up more.

Madeleines are best served warm, with whipped cream, sprinkled with powdered sugar, dipped in chocolate, with a custard, with coffee or tea, with jam or with a fruit salad.

Chocolate Mousse
Mousse au chocolat

I do not enjoy the consistency and diluted flavor of chocolate mousse made with whipped cream or gelatin. Adding a little unsalted butter helps to make the mousse a little firmer and sets off the rich flavor I prefer.

For me a dark chocolate has a more intense flavor, but you can also make a mousse with white or milk chocolate.

Serves 6 to 8   Intermediate

- 4 ounces bittersweet or semi-sweet chocolate (113 grams)
- ¼ stick unsalted butter (28 grams)
- ¼ cup granulated sugar (50 grams)
- 4 large eggs, separated
- 1 pinch of salt
- 1 teaspoon of coffee, vanilla extract, or Grand Marnier liqueur

Needed

- Double boiler
- Spatula
- 2 mixing bowls
- Stand or handheld mixer

1) In a gently simmering double boiler, melt the chocolate and the butter. Do not overheat.

2) When the chocolate is almost melted, remove from the heat, and stir with a spatula until smooth. Let cool.

3) In a bowl, beat with a whisk, a handheld mixer or stand mixer, the egg yolks, and the sugar until pale yellow in color and until it forms a ribbon when you scoop it out with a spoon.

4) Stir in the cooled chocolate gradually and the flavoring.

5) In a separate bowl, beat the egg whites with the salt until stiff peaks form. If I can turn the bowl of firmly beaten egg whites, upside down over my head without getting wet, I know the egg whites are stiff enough.

6) Fold ⅓ of the whites into the chocolate mixture with a spatula. Then, fold the rest gradually, until no whites are showing.

7) The mousse can be transferred to individual bowls, parfait glasses, or a big glass bowl. Refrigerate for at least 3 hours. You should obtain a creamy mousse. I have kept mousses in the fridge overnight and up to 24 hours. Yes, I dare say, and it will still taste like a real mousse but spongy. It depends on what kind of texture you like.

8) If you happen to have water at the bottom of your bowl, it is because you did not beat your egg whites stiff enough.

9) Serve plain or with whipped cream or a dry cookie like a sablé.

Tips

To obtain firm egg whites, make sure there is no yolk in the egg whites when you break them. If you do, your egg whites will never become firm, and you will have water in your mousse.

You also need to make sure your glass, copper or stainless steel bowl is clean and dry before whipping the egg whites.

Nougat Ice Cream

Nougat glacé

My dad, who enjoyed making desserts when he was retired, and had a sweet tooth, really loved to make this one, especially when they had friends over for coffee in the afternoon. He got the recipe from a friend and could not wait to try it on us. I make it regularly around the holidays.

Serves 6 to 8   Intermediate

Ice cream

- 3 large eggs
- 1½ cups whipping cream
- ½ cup granulated sugar (120 grams)
- ¼ cup raw honey (100 grams)
- ⅔ cup sliced almonds (100 grams)
- ¾ cup pecans (100 grams)
- ½ cup pistachios (75 grams)

- A handful each of dried cranberries and dried apricots that have been marinated in ⅛ cup rum or cranberries juice the night before

Berry coulis

- 2 cups raspberries (246 grams) or strawberries (290 grams)
- 2 tablespoons granulated sugar (25 grams)

Needed

- Frying pan
- Wooden spoon
- Stand or handheld mixer
- 2 medium size mixing bowls
- Largest mixing bowl you have
- Spatula
- Rectangular quick bread mold 9x4, half sphere mold, or individual muffin molds
- 3 to 4 rectangular strips of foil or plastic wrap 3x12
- Mixer/food processor or blender
- 2 small saucepans

Prepare ice cream

1) Chill bowl and beaters before mixing.

2) Roast the nuts in a frying pan, pour 1 to 2 tablespoons sugar on top and let caramelize. Keep stirring, with a wooden spoon so the nuts are well coated and caramelized. Watch them closely since they can burn fast. Cool and chop.

3) Separate the egg whites from the yolks. Boil the honey.

4) In a clean and dry medium size bowl, beat the egg whites until stiff peaks form and add the hot honey slowly as you continue beating.

5) In a large mixing bowl add the rest of the sugar to the egg yolks and beat until a thick pale-yellow ribbon drips from a lifted spoon. Gradually fold in the egg whites, by thirds using a spatula.

6) Beat the whipping cream in a medium size bowl until stiff peaks form and fold gently into egg sugar mixture.

7) Add the nuts and dried fruit to the mixture. Fold gently.

8) Use the foil/plastic wrap strips that will line the mold. Oil only the parts of the strips that are facing the ice cream. The foil strips will help you lift the ice cream from the mold.

9) Place the mixture in the mold on top of the strips. You can also freeze the mixture in individual molds for individual portions.

10) Cover with plastic wrap. Place in the freezer at least 12 hours before serving.

11) When ready to serve, unmold the nougat by lifting the strips. Place on a rectangular plate. Slice the rectangular cake and serve with the cold coulis in a sauce boat, on the side.

Prepare berry coulis

1) Chop the washed fruit and blend with the sugar.

2) Cook on the stove for a few minutes. Cool in the fridge.

Tips

If you can find glazed Australian apricots, they would be perfect for this recipe.

If you are having difficulties to unmold, gently dip the bottom of the mold in warm water and the nougat should unmold easily, when you turn the mold upside down on a plate.

Unserved portion can be kept for up to a week if frozen.

Grand Marnier Soufflé
Soufflé au Grand Marnier

As my mom used to say: "le soufflé n'attend pas, ce sont les convives qui attendent le soufflé" or "The soufflé waits for no one, it is the guests who wait for the soufflé." While this recipe from my dad is simpler than most, its success depends on having everything ready to go in advance but no longer than 30 minutes ahead. As with any soufflé, make it at the last minute!

Serves 4 to 5   Intermediate

For a 4-cup soufflé dish

- 5 large eggs at room temperature and separated
- ½ cup granulated sugar (100 grams)
- 1 pinch of salt for the egg whites
- 2 or 3 tablespoons of Grand Marnier liqueur or Cointreau
- ⅛ cup grated orange zest – the zest of 1 orange (optional)
- Softened butter and granulated sugar; about a tablespoon of each for pan

prep

- Powdered sugar to sprinkle

Needed

- Cookie sheet
- Pastry brush
- Parchment paper and a string
- Stand mixer
- 2 large mixing bowls
- Spatula
- 4-cup soufflé dish or four 8 to 10-ounce individual soufflé ramequins

1) Preheat oven with cookie sheet to 450°F.
2) Brush the sides of the soufflé dish or individual ramekins with softened butter then sprinkle granulated sugar inside and roll to cover the sides evenly. Pour out excess.
3) If you think your soufflé dish is going to be filled to the top, butter and sugar a parchment paper collar and tie it with a string around the soufflé dish top part so your soufflé has room to rise.
4) In a bowl, beat 5 egg yolks with ½ cup of granulated sugar. Beat at high speed until pale yellow in color and thick. Add the Grand Marnier and the zest if using.
5) In a clean and dry bowl beat the egg whites with a pinch of salt until stiff and add the 2 tablespoons of sugar towards the end. The egg whites should be shiny and not too stiff, but they should form peaks.
6) Fold the egg whites into the yolks gradually, by thirds, with a spatula.
7) Place the mixture in a soufflé dish or individual soufflé dishes. It should be ¾ full. Place the soufflé dish/dishes on top of the hot cookie sheet.
8) Bake for 10 to 12 minutes for single soufflé dish and about 6 to 8 minutes for individual dishes.

9) Remove from oven and sprinkle top with powdered sugar.

Tips

The difficulty in making a soufflé is how you organize yourself. If a soufflé waits even 15 minutes too long, when it comes out of the oven, it will collapse. The soufflé must cook the exact time. Prepare everything ahead of time, pour the mixture into the soufflé dish at the last minute and put it in the oven.

Always put the soufflé dish on a hot cookie sheet to speed up the rising.

Do not open the oven!! No peeking!

Apricot Tart

Tarte aux abricots

Every summer, we would make this tart on a puff pastry or a regular pastry crust. You can buy the readymade puff pastry or make your own. Puff pastry is best for apricots because it will hold up better with a juicy fruit. This is an easy tart to make.

Serves 6 to 8   Intermediate

- 1 pound fresh apricots washed at least 10 to 12 apricots (450grams)
- 1 or 2 tablespoons granulated sugar (12 to 13 grams)
- 1 sheet frozen puff pastry dough preferably made with butter defrosted in the fridge overnight then at room temperature for about 20 minutes
- Extra granulated sugar to sprinkle at the end

Needed

- A paring knife
- A rolling pin
- A 8 to 10 inches diameter tart pan, if possible, with removable bottom or a rectangular metal mold
- A serving plate

1) Cut the apricots in half and remove the pits.
2) Preheat the oven to 425°F.
3) Butter the metal tart pan if using.

4) Cut a circle of the rolled puff pastry until you can cover the pan. Line the bottom and the sides of the tart pan with the dough.

5) Place the apricots cut side facing up on the dough. Sprinkle with sugar.

6) Bake for 25 to 30 minutes on the middle rack.

7) Sprinkle with extra granulated sugar as it comes out of the oven.

8) Unmold when it has cooled.

Tips

This recipe is a little tart and can be sweetened with more sugar or served with a choice of vanilla ice cream, sweetened and flavored whipped cream.

Apple Tart or Apple Galette
Tarte ou Galette aux pommes

This is a great end to a fall or Thanksgiving dinner, light, not too sweet and delicious!

This pie dough is something between a cookie dough and a bread dough! I like to use ingredients that are very cold (butter, water) so the flour will cook faster than the butter.

You can either put the dough in a tart pan with a removable bottom or put it on a cookie sheet and give it a free form like a galette.

Serves up to 8   Intermediate

Pastry

- 1 cup flour (120 grams)
- 6 tablespoons cold unsalted butter (85 grams)
- ⅛ teaspoon salt
- 6 tablespoons ice-cold water
- ¼ cup sugar to sprinkle on the apples (50 grams)

- 3 tablespoons unsalted butter cut in small pieces and place on the fruit (43 grams)
- 1 egg yolk plus 2 teaspoons water for egg wash glaze (optional)

Filling

- 4 Golden Delicious apples
- Juice of ½ a lemon (optional)

Glaze

- 3 tablespoons apricot jam or red currant jelly
- 1½ tablespoons of rum or Cognac

Needed

- Pastry blender
- Medium mixing bowl
- Rolling pin
- 9 to 10-inch tart mold or a cookie sheet buttered
- Paring knife
- Small saucepan for the glaze
- Pastry brush

1) Preheat the oven to 400°F.
2) With a pastry blender, mix the flour, salt and the cold cut up butter in a bowl.
3) Gradually add the ice-cold water and mix with your hands until it forms a ball. Do not overwork the dough. Pieces of butter will show but that does not matter.
4) On a floured surface, roll the dough with a rolling pin to an 11-inch circle and place in a buttered 10-inch tart mold. Make sure the dough covers the sides too. If you want to make a free form galette, place the dough on a cookie sheet. Refrigerate at this point for about 15 to 20 minutes.

5) Peel 4 Golden Delicious apples. Cut them in quarters. Slice them, not too thin and place them in circles on the tart dough. Overlap each slice. I try to work quickly so, I do not need to put lemon on the apple slices, but if you are afraid the slices will turn brown, you could mix them in the juice of ½ lemon, before placing them on the tart dough. You can use the end pieces to form the center of the tart. Place them next to each other. If you are left with some slices, stick them in between the others or eat them!!

6) Sprinkle with sugar and add butter cubes here and there on the apples. If you decide to make the galette, you can fold the sides of the dough over the apples. If you want, you could use an egg wash-- egg yolk and water to brush on the folded dough, so it is golden when it bakes.

7) Bake for 40 to 50 minutes depending on your oven or until golden.

8) Combine the glaze ingredients when the tart comes out of the oven. Warm the mixture so it is fluid and brush the entire top of the tart.

Tips

If you work the dough too long, you are putting the gluten at work, therefore making the dough elastic. If you add more water, the humidity will also make the dough elastic.

In both cases, you end up with a tough dough. The secret is to work the dough as little as possible, to have a crunchy crust.

The sides of the tart may fall for the following reasons:

- Because the dough is too soft (too much water)
- Because the oven is not warm enough
- Because the room is too warm, or you softened the butter by working the dough too long.

Strawberry Tart

Tarte aux fraises

I remember those delicious strawberry tarts with a shortbread or sablé crusts and crème pâtissière in the French pâtisseries. In the Pacific Northwest every end of May or early June the strawberries are plentiful and delicious so, it is time to make a tart! This recipe takes a little time, but the result is worth the time and effort! Delicious!

The pastry and pastry cream can be made the day ahead. Assemble all the components and glaze a few hours before serving.

Serves 8 persons   Advanced

For the pastry

- ½ cup unsalted butter at room temperature (113 grams)
- 6 tablespoons ground almond or almond flour (50 grams)
- ¼ cup sugar (50 grams)
- ¼ teaspoon salt
- ⅛ teaspoon almond extract
- 1 cup white all-purpose flour (120 grams)

Needed

- Stand mixer, handheld mixer, or a food processor
- Measuring cups and spoons
- Wooden spoon
- Wax paper or plastic wrap
- Rolling pin

- ➢ 9-inch tart pan with a removable bottom

1) Beat the butter in a mixer until white and fluffy.
2) Add the ground almonds, sugar, and salt. Continue beating until well mixed. Add the almond extract.
3) With a wooden spoon, work in the flour until the dough is soft and smooth. If you have a food processor this might help the process. You should have a ball of dough. Wrap it in plastic wrap or wax paper.
4) Refrigerate the dough for 30 minutes.
5) Roll the dough between two sheets of wax paper into a 10-inch circle. Remove the top sheet of wax paper and flip the dough onto the 9-inch tart pan with a removable bottom. Press the pastry onto the bottom and the sides. You can use pieces of dough to repair certain areas that might be thinner than others.
6) Preheat the oven to 350°F.
7) Refrigerate the tart shell 30 minutes.
8) Bake 20 minutes or until golden. Cool completely on a wire rack then remove part of the mold, keeping the tart on the bottom piece.

Pastry cream

- 3 large egg yolks
- ½ cup sugar (100 grams)
- ¼ cup white all-purpose flour (31 grams)
- 1 cup scalded milk
- ½ teaspoon vanilla, rum, or almond extract
- 1 tablespoon butter (14 grams)

Needed

- ➢ Stand or handheld mixer

- ➢ A medium saucepan
- ➢ A wooden spoon
- ➢ Plastic wrap

1) Beat the egg yolks and the sugar in a bowl until the mixture becomes thick and forms a ribbon when you dip a wooden spoon in it and lift it up.
2) Stir in the flour. Mix well.
3) Stir in milk that has been scalded to 180°F gradually to temper the eggs, so they do not scramble. Then pour the whole mixture back into a saucepan.
4) Heat the mixture stirring constantly with a wooden spoon until boiling. Boil for 2 minutes.
5) Take off the heat and whisk until cool for 2 or 3 minutes.
6) Stir in the vanilla. Stir in the butter that will melt and prevent a skin from forming.
7) Cover with a plastic wrap and refrigerate.

Fruit glaze

- 2 pints of hulled, washed, and dried strawberries
- ⅓ cup strawberry jam or jelly
- 1 or 1½ tablespoons of rum or Cognac

Needed

- ➢ Saucepan
- ➢ Pastry brush

Assembly

1) When the tart shell has cooled, fill with pastry cream.
2) Arrange the whole strawberries on top of the cream.

3) Prepare the glaze by melting the jam or jelly with the flavoring, in a saucepan, on medium heat. Stir with a wooden spoon until all the jam/jelly is dissolved. Brush on the glaze with a pastry brush. Eventually the glaze will solidify and give the brilliant look wprofessional tarts have.

Tips

You can make the tart shell and the pastry cream the day before and assemble at the last minute.

Raspberry Tartlets
Tartelettes aux framboises

If you buy strawberry or raspberry tarts in a pâtisserie, or eat them in a restaurant in France, you will notice that they always have a sweet crust, like a shortbread.

The fruit can be right on the crust or more often it is on top of a pastry cream. Sometimes, it is on top of a whipped cream or a crème fraiche filling. Choose the filling you prefer.

They are always topped with a raspberry or redcurrant glaze.

These are my favorite dessert!

Serves 6 to 8   Advanced

Shortbread

- 1¼ cup all-purpose flour (160 grams)
- 1 dash salt
- 6 tablespoons unsalted butter at room temperature (85 grams)
- ⅔ cup granulated sugar (130 grams)

- 1 large egg yolk
- 1 tablespoon vanilla, rum, or almond extract

Needed

- ➢ Food processor, handheld, or a stand mixer
- ➢ 14 small tartlets molds, non-stick metal
- ➢ Fork
- ➢ Plastic wrap

1) Preheat the oven to 400°F.
2) Pour the flour in the food processor. Add the softened butter, sugar, and salt. Pulse and mix well until creamy. Add one egg yolk and pulse and mix until well blended. Work the dough as little as possible to avoid toughening. Make a ball and wrap with plastic wrap.
3) Refrigerate for one hour if possible. This way the butter will harden, causing the rest of the dough to bake faster than the butter melts, making a crunchier crust.
4) Allow about 1 or 2 tablespoons of dough per mold. Press into the molds and up the sides with your fingers. Prick with a fork a couple of times, at least.
5) Bake for 10 to 15 minutes or until lightly browned. Cool in the pan then invert the molds by tapping lightly the bottom to unmold.

Pastry cream

- 3 large egg yolks
- ½ cup granulated sugar (100 grams)
- ¼ cup all-purpose flour (31 grams)
- 1 cup scalded milk, heat just below boiling, 180°F
- ½ teaspoon vanilla, rum, or almond extract

- 1 tablespoon of butter (14 grams)

Needed

- Medium bowl
- Medium saucepan
- Small saucepan
- Wooden spoon
- Plastic wrap

1) Scald milk by bringing it to 180°F, just below boiling indicated by small bubbles forming along the edge of pan and first signs of steam.

2) Beat the egg yolks and the sugar in a medium bowl until thick, pale yellow in color, and forming ribbon when you lift a spoon that was dipped in the mixture.

3) Stir in the flour and mix well, then gradually add scalded milk and the flavoring. Mix until smooth.

4) Transfer to a medium saucepan and heat the mixture to boiling, stirring constantly on medium heat until thick.

5) Add the flavoring off the heat.

6) Keep stirring for another 2 minutes with the butter, off the heat to prevent a skin to form when cool. Cover with a plastic wrap and refrigerate. It makes 1⅓ cup of pastry cream.

Crème fraîche instead of pastry cream

- 1 cup whipping cream (48 grams)
- 1 tablespoon sour cream (12 grams)

Needed

- Small mixing bowl

1) Mix the two ingredients. Warm up at 90 to 100°F. Leave covered on the kitchen counter overnight.

2) Refrigerate for up to two weeks.

3) Use about a tablespoon or two of crème to cover the crust, then arrange the fruits on top and finally brush on the glaze. It makes over a cup of crème fraiche.

Assembly

1) Fill the crust with one or two tablespoons of your pastry cream or crème fraîche at the last minute and place the raspberries on top.

2) Apply the glaze, see recipe below. This should be done in the last 30 minutes before serving or the crust will become soggy.

For the glaze

- 3 or 4 tablespoons red currant or raspberry jelly (50 to 65 grams)
- 1½ to 2 tablespoon kirsch liqueur, dark rum, or water

Needed

- Small saucepan
- Wooden spoon
- Pastry brush

1) Blend the jelly with the liquid in a small saucepan and place the pan on medium heat. Keep stirring with a wooden spoon.

2) When the jelly is all melted use a pastry brush to apply the glaze on the fruit just before serving. The fruits will be shiny and appetizing.

Almond Juiles

Juiles aux amandes

We used to make these often as kids because they only had 5 ingredients and did not require a special technique. Easy for kids to make. They are a great light and crispy cookie that looks more difficult to make than it is. They are elegant served with ice cream, sorbet, fruit salad or a cream dessert or simply with coffee or tea in the afternoon.

Tuiles means tiles because when finished, they resemble the tiles on a roof.

Yields 30 to 32   Easy

- ¼ cup sugar (50 grams)
- 4 tablespoons white flour (31 grams)
- 2 large egg whites
- 2½ tablespoons melted butter (35 grams)
- 4½ tablespoons sliced almonds (40 grams)

Needed

- Mixing bowl
- Stand mixer or handheld mixer
- Baking sheet with parchment paper
- Small coffee or teaspoon
- Rolling pin
- Offset metal spatula

1) Preheat the oven to 350°F.

2) Beat the egg whites till slightly foaming. Mix in the sugar gradually, then the flour and pour the melted butter. The mixture will be foaming and runny.

3) On prepared baking sheet drop teaspoons of batter about 1-2 inches apart. Flatten each dollop with the back of a spoon.

4) Sprinkle sliced almonds on top of each circle of dough.

5) Bake on the middle rack, for 8 to 10 minutes until slightly golden brown on the edges while the center looks baked but still cream color.

6) As soon as you can handle them, use an offset spatula to lift them out and place them on a rolling pin right side up so they get a curved shape. Make sure you block the rolling pin to keep it in place. Let cool. They will be crispy and light! Careful, they might break easily.

Tips

They are fragile and will lose their crispness in a humid environment. To store them use a large metal box. You can leave them flat for storage.

Holiday Dishes

Apple Yam Bake 224
Christmas Yule Log 226
Christmas Crown with Salmon 230
Christmas Candies 233
Chocolate Dipped Apricots 234
Christmas Chocolates 236
Marzipan Stuffed Dried Fruits 238
Mendiants 240
Rochers 243
Chocolate Truffles 244
Epiphany or Kings Cake 247

Apple Yam Bake

When I came to the United States, our American mom invited us to celebrate the American holiday of Thanksgiving which falls on the 4th Thursday of November. Maxine Kopczynski used to tell me, "This is actually the only day when Americans eat better than the French!" Well, Thanksgiving being a Thursday, she might have had a point since for French people there was nothing special happening on the fourth Thursday of November.

One of the standard side dishes that she made, and I love, is an Apple Yam Bake.

Serves 8 to 10   Easy

- 2 pounds yams, can substitute sweet potatoes (900 grams)
- 1½ pounds apples (675 grams)
- ⅔ cup brown sugar (130 grams)
- 6 tablespoons unsalted butter (85 grams)
- ½ cup orange or apple juice
- 3 tablespoons maple syrup
- 1 tablespoon lemon juice

- 1 teaspoon cinnamon
- ½ teaspoon ginger

Needed

- 2 saucepans (one large and one small)
- Paring knife
- 8x11 buttered baking dish

1) Preheat oven to 350°F.
2) Place yams unpeeled in a large saucepan. Cover with water and bring to a boil. Reduce to simmer and cook until barely tender.
3) Peel, core, and slice the apples.
4) Once cooked, peel the yams and cut discs but not too thin circles.
5) In a buttered gratin or baking dish, alternate circles of yams with slices of apples.
6) In a small saucepan, mix sugar, butter, juice, maple syrup, cinnamon, ginger and bring to a boil then simmer for 10 minutes.
7) Pour the sauce over the arranged yams and apples.
8) Place the dish in the oven and cook for about 30 minutes.

Christmas Yule Log
Bûche de Noël

In France you hardly think of making a Yule log since they are readymade in pastry shops and they have so many varieties and flavors.

When I came to the US in the '70s these were a hard commodity to find. So, I toiled over that dessert and tried so many times that I was ready to quit. Finally, I combined different recipes and made it my own. Now, I am satisfied with the finished product that took years of labor!

Serves up to 12   Advanced

Cake

- 4 large eggs separated at room temperature with no yolk in the whites
- ½ cup granulated sugar (100 grams)
- 1 teaspoon pure vanilla extract
- 8 tablespoons all purpose white flour (60 grams)
- ⅛ teaspoon salt

Needed

- 9x13 greased cookie sheet
- Parchment or wax paper
- Stand or handheld mixer
- Measuring cups and spoons
- Large mixing bowls
- 2 spatulas one metal
- Cloth towel sprinkled with powdered sugar

1) Preheat the oven to 375°F.
2) Grease cookie sheet and line it with parchment/wax paper. Butter and flour the parchment/wax paper.
3) In a mixing bowl, beat 4 egg yolks with ½ cup of sugar at medium speed, until thick and pale lemon yellow in color. Add 1 teaspoon of vanilla, 8 tablespoons of flour and the salt. Mix gently at this point.
4) In a different clean dry bowl whip the egg whites until stiff. Fold them lightly in the cake batter with a spatula, one third at a time.
5) Spread the dough about ½ inch thick on the cookie sheet.
6) Bake for about 8 minutes on the center rack. Do not overbake or the cake will crack when rolled.
7) Slide the cake off the baking sheet onto a rack by pulling the wax paper with the cake on top.
8) Invert the cake on a cloth towel sprinkled with powdered sugar. Remove the paper, roll up the hot cake with the towel, and let cool for 30 minutes.

Buttercream divided

- 4 large egg yolks
- 9 tablespoons granulated sugar (113 grams)

- ⅓ cup water
- 1 cup unsalted butter at room temperature (230 grams)
- 3 ounces semi-sweet chocolate (85 grams)
- 1½ tablespoons of Grand-Marnier divided

Needed

- Small saucepan
- Medium bowl
- Double boiler
- Offset spatula
- Sharp knife and fork
- Christmas decorations

1) In a medium bowl, beat 4 egg yolks just until mixed.
2) In a small saucepan, heat the sugar with the water until dissolved. Bring it to a boil until the syrup reaches soft-ball stage, 239°F on a candy thermometer. Wait 20 seconds until bubbles in the syrup subside.
3) Gradually add the hot syrup to the egg mixture in a thin stream while beating constantly. Pour the syrup between the beaters and the bowl. The hot syrup should not stick to either. Beat as fast as possible until the mixture thickens and cools.
4) Cream the butter by adding it gradually into the egg yolk/syrup mixture which must be quite cool, or the butter will melt.
5) Add ½ tablespoon Grand Marnier to buttercream and then divide in two equal parts.
6) Melt the coarsely chopped chocolate in a double boiler. Cool slightly.
7) Add the melted chocolate to one part and an additional tablespoon Grand Marnier to the other part.

Tips

Butter cream can be prepared up to 3 days ahead, covered and refrigerated. To spread it you will have to leave it at room temperature for a while.

Sugar syrup

- ½ cup granulated sugar (100 grams)
- ⅓ cup water

Needed

➢ Small saucepan and pastry brush

1) Combine sugar and water in saucepan.
2) Bring to a boil for 1 or 2 minutes until clear. Cool and set aside.

To assemble

1) Unroll the cooked cake and brush with the sugar syrup.
2) Using the offset spatula spread the Grand Marnier buttercream on the cake.
3) Roll up the cake, removing the towel as you roll. Trim each end of the rolled cake with a sharp knife. These cake trimmings should be rolled tightly into spirals so they can be attached later to the log as wood knots.
4) With a little chocolate buttercream, attach the trimmings to the log.
5) Use the remaining chocolate buttercream to frost the log and knots with a spatula then use a fork to mark lines to resemble the bark of a log.
6) To make the chocolate smooth on each end of the log, dip a metal spatula into hot water and spread the hot spatula on the chocolate covered ends in one movement from bottom to top.
7) Decorate with holiday trimmings: Santa on a sleigh, reindeers, fir trees, nativity scenes, angels, stars. Refrigerate up to 1 or 2 days.

For a more finished touch you can sprinkle some confectioner's sugar to imitate snow on a log!

Christmas Crown with Salmon

Couronne de Noël au Saumon

It is hard to find a Christmas dish that requires little preparation, easy to find ingredients, yet looks festive and pleases everyone.

In 2019, my family decided to go to France for the holidays. I discovered this recipe, and it was a hit with everyone. I served it for Christmas brunch, but it could be served for lunch or dinner with a salad.

It has become a classic in my family!

Serves 8   Intermediate

- 1 tablespoon of unsalted butter and oil
- 4 sliced leeks about 1⅓ pound (600 grams)
- ½ to ¾ cup crumbled feta cheese (75 to 100 grams)
- 1 tablespoon sour cream or crème fraiche
- 1 sheet of frozen puff pastry preferably with butter
- ½ to ¾ pound salmon cut in cubes (225 to 340 grams)

- Dill (optional)
- 1 large egg yolk
- 1 tablespoon milk
- 1 tablespoon sesame seeds (optional)
- Salt and pepper

Needed

- Frying pan
- Rolling pin
- 9-inch tart pan with a removable bottom buttered
- Bowl approximately 6-inch diameter
- Small knife
- Medium mixing bowl
- Small mixing bowl
- Pastry brush
- Large serving platter

1) Preheat oven to 400°F.

2) Cook the sliced leeks until soft in a little butter and oil. Add the cream, feta. Salt and pepper to taste.

3) To form the pastry ring on a lightly floured surface, roll out the puff pastry dough with a lightly floured rolling pin. It should be a circle of about 10 inches. Place it in a tart pan covering the bottom and the sides.

4) Place the 6-inch bowl upside down in the middle of the dough lined tart pan. Press down with enough force to leave a circular impression being careful not to cut through the dough. Remove the small bowl and make 4 equally spaced diagonal cuts that go from edge to edge of circular impression by passing through the center point of the circle. The first cut should bisect the circle in half, the second will produce 4 equal quarters, the final two cuts should divide each quarter equally so that you have 8 equal seg-

ments that will eventually be folded back to partially cover the filling.

5) Place the leeks mixture on the ring of dough formed between the circular impression and edge of the tart pan.

6) Sprinkle salt and pepper and dill on the salmon cubes in a small bowl. Mix well and place them on top of the leeks.

7) Close the triangles by folding them over the leeks/salmon mixture and gluing the points of the triangles on the dough with some egg yolk mixed with the milk.

8) Brush the rest of the egg yolk milk wash on the whole dough so it has a nice glaze when it comes out of the oven.

9) Sprinkle with sesame seeds.

10) Bake for 30 to 40 minutes.

11) Serve, removing the edges of the tart pan and placing the couronne on the removable bottom directly on the large platter.

Christmas Candies

Friandises de Noël

For me, Christmas and New Year means visions of marzipan treats such as dates, prunes and walnut halves stuffed with colored marzipan, or dried apricots dipped in dark chocolate, prunes stuffed with blanched almonds, chocolate/almond rochers, chocolate candies filled with liqueur, dried fruits or nuts.

Often at Christmas my dad would bring home huge chocolate boxes, gifted by his suppliers. As kids, we were impatient to look under the lid to see how many layers of chocolates were there. Sometimes the boxes were so stuffed with chocolates that the lid could not close and it was held together with a huge ribbon.

For most of the confectioners' shops and pâtisseries in France, the end of the year is the busiest time of the year. The customers line up to buy all sorts of delicious treats to celebrate end of the year festivities. I hope you like these treats as much as I do!

Chocolate Dipped Apricots

Abricots au chocolat

Yield 24   Easy

- 24 candied Australian apricots or dried apricots if you cannot find the candied ones
- 4 ounces dark chocolate, or 2 ounces dark and 2 ounces bitter chocolate (115 grams)

Needed

- ➢ Double boiler
- ➢ Wooden spoon
- ➢ Candy thermometer
- ➢ Parchment paper
- ➢ 24 mini paper candy cups

1) Melt the chocolate in a double boiler. Cool until the temperature on the candy thermometer shows 80 to 90°F. The chocolate should be thick

enough to dip the apricots.

2) Dip half of one apricot in the lukewarm chocolate and continue with the others. Place each apricot on parchment paper. When they are cooled and the chocolate has hardened then place them in the paper candy cups.

3) You can refrigerate up to 3 weeks in an airtight container.

Christmas Chocolates
Chocolats de Noël

Yieds 24 chocolates   Intermediate

- 4 ounces dark chocolate (115 grams)
- 24 maraschino cherries, or 24 hazelnuts, other nut or pralines

Ganache

- 6 ounces dark chocolate (173 grams)
- ¼ cup sour cream (48 grams)
- 1 to 2 tablespoons instant espresso

Needed

- Double boiler
- 24 mini paper candy cups
- Pastry bag with small star tip or soup spoon

1) Melt the 4 ounces chocolate in a double boiler. Stir with a wooden spoon until almost melted. Remove from heat, it will continue to melt. Mix well until smooth.

2) Place a teaspoon of the chocolate in a paper candy cup. Place a cherry or a nut on top. Press hard on the chocolate. Refrigerate while preparing ganache.

3) Make the ganache by melting the 6 ounces dark chocolate in a double-boiler. Turn off the heat as the chocolate is almost melted. It will continue melting as you stir with a spoon. When cooled, add the sour cream and the instant espresso powder. If you like coffee add the 2 tablespoons but for a milder flavor, use only 1 tablespoon.

4) If you are lazy, take a soup spoon and some of the ganache and place it on top of the cherry or nut in the mini paper candy cup. To give it a professional look, wait until the chocolate cools to a thick consistency. You can then use a pastry bag fitted with a small star tip to apply the ganache on top of filling in each candy cup.

Marzipan Stuffed Dried Fruits
Fruits déguisés

I remember the sweets we had for Christmas in France while growing up! Oodles of chocolate truffles, rochers with almonds, chocolates filled with liqueurs and marzipan delicacies. What a delight!

We eat well during the holidays in France. We used to make these at home but of course now marzipan delicacies are found in pastry shops around France!

Makes 24+   Easy

- 16 ounces marzipan (450 grams)
- Prunes
- Dates
- Walnut halves
- Food coloring

Needed

➢ Paring knife

➢ 24 mini paper candy cups

1) Knead the marzipan and divide into 3 balls. Color each ball with a different food coloring. Just one drop will be enough for each ball. You can do pink for prunes, green for dates and yellow for walnuts.

2) Cut the prunes and the dates in half and remove the pits. Take a little ball of marzipan, shape it like a finger and stuff it in the dried fruit. Then close

the fruit around the marzipan.

3) Take 2 walnut halves and make a little ball of marzipan. Press the two halves on each side of the ball.

4) Repeat and fill all the mini paper candy cups with the *fruits déguisés*. Save in a metal box for Christmas.

Mendiants

Mendicants

These chocolate candies are part of the Provençal Christmas. I discovered these in Annecy, at Christmas time and it has been a favorite ever since, in our family. They are a specialty mostly in the Occitan region of Southern France. It is a tradition dating back to the Middle Ages, when you had a gros souper –a big dinner on Christmas Eve before midnight mass. At the end of the dinner, there were 13 desserts as a remembrance of the 12 apostles and Jesus.

One of these desserts was the Mendiants. These delicacies have 4 dried fruits and nuts (Malaga raisins, hazelnuts, blanched almonds, and dried figs of Provence), that represent the 4 religious orders of the Middle Ages church. The monks of a mendicant order devote themselves only to prayer and survive exclusively through the charity of others.

The four mendicant orders are:

> *The Franciscans dressed in dark brown and represented by the Malaga raisin*
>
> *The Carmes dressed in light brown and represented by the hazelnut*
>
> *The Dominicans dressed in white and represented by the blanched almond*
>
> *The Augustins dressed in purple represented by the dried fig of Provence.*

This is how chocolate Mendicants got their name. Who would imagine that such a chocolate candy could be so spiritual and full of symbols!

Yields 15 to 20 Mendicants depending on the size.

- 4 or 5 ounces semi-sweet chocolate (113 to 142 grams)
- 4 or 5 ounces milk chocolate or white chocolate (113 to 142 grams)
- Dried fruit and nuts (dried cranberries, raisins, dried apricots, blanched almonds, pecans, hazelnuts, walnuts)
- Marzipan or almond paste

Needed

- 2 double boiler saucepans or 2 bowls for the microwave
- Candy thermometer
- Parchment paper and tray
- Pencil and a glass or round cookie cutter
- Tablespoon

1) Melt the two chocolates separately in double boilers or in the microwave in segment of 30 seconds at a time.
2) To temper the chocolate, it should not exceed 120°F. Mix well and let it cool until the temperature reaches 83°F Fahrenheit. This will allow the chocolate to remain shiny, not melt in your hands, not discolor, and make a clean cut when you break it, after it hardens.
3) When the two melted chocolates look smooth and shiny, on a piece of parchment paper, trace some circles with a pencil using a glass or a cookie cutter.
4) With a tablespoon, take some melted chocolate and spread the chocolate around in the circles, with the back of the spoon, trying to fill the circles.
5) When the chocolates are spread in the circles, add pieces of nuts, dried fruit, or marzipan.
6) Let cool in the fridge for 1 to 2 hours. They will lift easily from the parchment paper before serving. You can keep them for a couple of weeks in the fridge in a metal box.

Rochers

Rochers des Monédières

This is an old recipe from my aunt Jeanne. She used to call these Rochers des Monédières after a mountain in the Limousin region in the southwest of France. She used half milk chocolate and half dark chocolate with slivered almonds. She would make mounds on parchment paper. I have adapted the recipe to me and my family's taste by using only dark chocolate.

Yields 24   Easy

- ⅔ cup blanched slivered almonds (110 grams)
- 8 ounces dark chocolate (230 grams)
- 2 tablespoons butter (28 grams)

Needed

- Cookie sheet or a frying pan
- Double boiler
- Wooden spoon
- Soup spoon
- Parchment paper

1) Preheat the oven to 400°F.
2) Place the almonds on a cookie sheet and toast them for 3 or 4 minutes until they are golden. You can do this in a dry frying pan so you can keep an eye on them more easily. Watch closely as they will burn very quickly.
3) Melt the chocolate and the butter in a double boiler pan. When the mix-

ture is smooth and almost melted add the grilled almonds.

4) Drop soup spoon size mounds of mixture on parchment paper.

5) Refrigerate for 40 minutes. Keep in an airtight container for 2 to 3 weeks.

Chocolate Truffles

Truffes au chocolat

This was a tradition at our house to have truffles during the holidays. In 1984, I entered my coffee chocolate truffles dipped in tempered chocolate and I won 3rd place behind 2 professional chocolatiers at the Oregon School of Arts and Crafts Chocolate Affair.

Makes 24   Intermediate

- 8 ounces dark chocolate (230 grams)
- ½ stick of unsalted butter at room temperature (55 grams)
- 3 tablespoons granulated sugar (45 grams)
- 2 large egg yolks
- 2 tablespoons rum, liquid coffee or Grand Marnier
- ½ cup ground almond (56 grams)
- 2 tablespoons cocoa powder (14 grams)
- 4 ounces melted chocolate (115 grams optional)

Needed
- Double boiler
- Wooden spoon
- Stand mixer
- Small mixing bowl
- Candy thermometer
- Fork
- Parchment paper

- 24 mini paper candy cups

1) Melt the chocolate in a double boiler. When it is almost all melted and the mixture is smooth, stir it up with a wooden spoon and put it aside to cool.

2) In a stand mixer, beat the butter and the sugar until you obtain a creamy mixture. Add the egg yolks, one at a time. Mix until smooth. Add flavoring and mix well.

3) When the chocolate is cooled add it to the butter and egg mixture. Mix on slow speed, adding the ground almond. Flatten the mixture into a 9 to 10 inch disc between two sheets of parchment paper. Refrigerate for 30 minutes.

4) After the mixture has hardened, take about a tablespoon of it and roll it in the palms of your hands. It should not be a perfect round ball but should ressemble the natural shape of a truffle mushroom.

5) Roll each truffle in cocoa powder and place in the paper candy cups.

6) It can be refrigerated in an airtight container for 2 to 3 weeks

Tips

If you want to dip the truffles in tempered chocolate, instead of cocoa powder, here is the recipe:

1) Melt the 4 ounces chocolate in a double boiler while you are rolling the truffles in the palm of your hands.

2) Cool the chocolate until it reaches the temperature of 80 to 90°F on a candy thermometer. The chocolate should be quite thick but still runny.

3) With a fork, dip the truffles, one at a time, in the lukewarm chocolate, drain the truffles and place on parchment or wax paper. Cool and refrigerate for several hours. When they are ready, you can place the truffles in the paper candy cups.

4) You can keep the chocolate covered truffles up to 3 weeks in a metal box in between parchment paper, in layers, in the fridge.

Oregon School of Arts and Crafts

FRANCINE CHOUGH

3ʀᴅ prize winner in the

CANDY/FUDGE

category

In the bake-off contest for the

Chocolate Affair

November 3, 1984

Mary Greeley
Director

Epiphany or Kings Cake
Galette des rois

Epiphany, on January 6th, is supposed to be the day the 3 kings visited baby Jesus in the manger. We celebrate this day in France by eating an almond paste galette with a small hidden bean or icon representing the baby Jesus. It is good luck for the person who finds it. Many people believe that it is a strategy from the pâtisseries and confectioners to prolong the holiday season during the month of January, an otherwise slow month for business for these shops. This galette is eaten mostly in the northern part of France. In the south, they celebrate this holiday by eating a brioche with candied fruit.

Even though we used to buy this galette at a pâtisserie, every year for this holiday, in France, I have recreated it with the help of my daughter, so I can make it at home in the USA.

My parents celebrated this holiday because it was low key. You buy a Kings galette at the local pâtisserie, and you invite friends in the afternoon, serving coffee or Champagne. Since this holiday is celebrated during the whole month of January and all the pâtisseries offer this delicacy all month, this is another opportunity to celebrate the New Year and be invited to friends' homes during January, an otherwise boring month.

When you buy it at the store, you get the galette with a couple gold crowns made from gold cardboard. Inside the galette, there is a little icon made of porcelain representing the baby Jesus and the person who finds it in his or her portion becomes the king or the queen for the day.

Serves 8 to 10   Intermediate

- A box of frozen puff pastry that contains two sheets

For the frangipane

- 1¼ cup almond flour (120 grams)
- ½ cup sugar (100 grams)
- 7 tablespoons cubed, unsalted butter at room temperature (100 grams)
- 2 large eggs
- 2 teaspoons rum or almond extract
- 3 teaspoons cornstarch (8 grams)

For the glaze

- 1 egg yolk mixed in a teaspoon of milk

Needed

- Rolling pin
- Mixing bowl or a stand mixer
- Cookie sheet
- Small baby Jesus made of porcelain, a whole almond, or a bean called the *fève*

1) Combine all the dry ingredients in the mixing bowl of a stand mixer. Incorporate the softened butter, beat well and then add the eggs one at a time. Add the flavoring. At the end, add the cornstarch.

2) Roll each sheet of puff pastry one at a time and cut circles of about 9 inches in diameter.

3) Preheat the oven to 375°F.

4) Butter a cookie sheet and place the first circle of dough on it. Put ½ to ⅔ of the almond paste, or all of it if you prefer, in the center and spread it around leaving about 1 inch of the edge not covered. Place the *fève* repre-

senting baby Jesus where it will be discovered in one of the slices.

5) Wet your finger with water and run it all around the edge. After you roll out your second circle, place it on top of the frangipane and press on the edges of the circles so the two circles are well glued together.

6) Poke about 4 to 6 holes on the top dough for the steam to escape.

7) With a knife you can score a design on the top, the most common being consecutive spirals. Look online for examples and ideas.

8) Scallop the edges all the way around the circle.

9) For the glaze, mix the egg yolk and milk and brush it on top of the galette. Do not brush the scalloped edges because it will prevent them from rising.

10) Bake for about 30 minutes. When golden, take out of the oven and let it rest. It is good lukewarm.

To serve, the parent cuts the galette in portions and the youngest child of the family goes under the table. The parent asks the child under the table: "Who gets this piece?" the child assigns the piece to one member of the party, not knowing who gets the *fève*. This way is a fair way of distributing pieces without knowing who gets to be king or queen.

Tips

Frangipane can be saved in the fridge for up to a week in an airtight container. Experiment to see how much frangipane you, and your family like as filling.

Drinks

Drinks and Beverages 252
Alcoholic Drinks 252
Non-alcoholic Drinks 256
Mineral Waters 257

Drinks and Beverages
Boissons

Wines and liqueurs are the most famous French alcoholic drinks, but there are also non-alcoholic drinks among them spring waters.

My uncle, Henri, had his own still to distill liqueurs and eaux de vie from fruits or fruit pits, for the whole village where he lived in the Limousin region. Licensed by the French government it was a special privilege in the 1950s and part of a tradition dating to the Napoléonic era. He could distill up to 20 liters of alcohol at 50 degrees (100 proof US), without paying taxes. He was bouilleur de cru—vintage distiller. This privilege does not exist anymore since now the bouilleur de cru would have to pay taxes on 50% to 100% of their production.

This is not an exhaustive list since there are many local and national drinks not listed here. These are the most known.

ALCOHOLIC DRINKS

Wines

Most of France is covered with vineyards except for Brittany, Normandy, the Hauts de France region and the Ile de France - Parisian region. There are reds, whites, rosés and Champagne or sparkling wines from different regions. Champagne comes only from the region of Champagne so, any other sparkling wine from another region cannot be called Champagne.

As children we were around wine. For lunch or dinner, we would drink water tinted with a drop of red wine. As we grew older, we would add a little bit more wine in the water. For big family banquets on a birthday, baptism, communion, wedding, or family celebrations we would get a taste of Champagne.

Kir and Kir Royale

Having grown up in Burgundy and gone to Dijon University, I was familiar with kir and the Kir Royale cocktail. The representative in the Assemblée Nationale and mayor of Dijon for over 20 years from 1945 to 1968 was Félix Kir, a catholic priest and cleric with the title of *Chanoine* or Canon. During the French occupation he was a resistance fighter who helped in the escape of over 5,000 prisoners of war. He became famous for his eponymous drink.

There used to be a local drink called *blanc cassis* which associated the local white wine with the local blackcurrant liqueur. Chanoine Kir liked to serve this drink to all the delegations who would visit him. He was also known to carry bottles of both drinks in his suitcase when he took the train to Paris. He would often share the drinks with the train passengers.

He was famous for his larger than life personality and his scathing repartees. In 1952, the Chanoine agreed to give his name to the local drink.

How to make your own kir or Kir Royale

For each glass:

- 1 volume of blackcurrant liqueur
- 2 volumes of white wine preferably Aligoté or Chardonnay
- Or 2 volumes of Crémant de Bourgogne if making a Kir Royale.

A votre santé!!

Cider/Calvados/Trou Normand

Normandy has lots of apples. Outside of the recipes that call for apples, like apple tart, Bourdelots, Chicken Vallée d'Auge, the Normands make a lot of cider.

Cidre Doux is a cider that has not fermented. *Cidre Brut* is a cider that has fermented and has some alcohol. If you ferment that cider even longer, you obtain Calvados an apple brandy.

Le Trou Normand, which means the Norman hole, was a pause in the middle of a long banquet and an excuse to drink Calvados. It was said to aid digestion and prepare your palate for the salad, cheese, and dessert courses. Nowadays, *Le Trou Normand* is served as an apple sorbet sprinkled with Calvados and julienned apples.

Pastis

In the region of Provence, life is a little slower. So, we take time to drink a Pastis before lunch or dinner as an aperitif. Pastis is an anise flavored drink which also may include several aromatic herbs among them, dill. The traditional drink, famous around the Marseille region, is prepared as follows:

- 1 volume of pastis
- 5 to 7 volumes of water.

The most famous brands are Pernod and Ricard. It is very refreshing under the southern heat!

Cognac and Armagnac

Cognac is a 40% alcoholic brandy produced in the Charentes region north of Bordeaux. It is distilled twice in copper pot stills then aged at least 2 years in French oak barrels. It is made with very dry white wine. Some can be aged for more than 14 years. It is an AOC protected product and must be made according to certain rules to be called Cognac. The most known brands are Courvoisier, Hennessy, Martell and Rémy Martin. Many drinks are based on Cognac: such as, Grand Marnier, Chambord, Sidecar for example.

Armagnac is the oldest brandy distilled in the world (1300). It has a 52% alcohol content. It is more fragrant and more flavorful than Cognac. It is distilled in oak barrels and made of 10 different grapes. It is also an AOC regulated product. That region is also in the southwest and south of the Cognac region.

Grand Marnier

This is an orange flavored liqueur created in 1880 in the west of Paris. It is a combination of Cognac and bitter oranges. You can drink it with water or on ice. In France it is considered a digestif, a post dinner drink. It is mostly used in cooking like in crepes Suzette or soufflés.

Bénédictine

This is another herbal digestif made with 27 herbs, spices, and peels. It is made by monks in Fécamp, Normandy. It is sweet and has undertones of licorice and honey. It dates to the 19th century.

A drier version called B&B was created in the 1930's, blending Bénédictine with Cognac. You can drink it as an after-dinner drink.

Cointreau

This liqueur was created in the 19th century near Angers, in the western region of Pays de la Loire. It is a triple sec liqueur made with mild and bitter orange peels. This is used as an aperitif, a digestif, and is an ingredient in cocktails.

Chartreuse

It is an herbal liqueur that was created in La Grande Chartreuse Monastery, near Grenoble by the Carthusian monks in 1737 according to instructions given to them in a manuscript dating to the 1600's. It is often used as a digestif. It is made of brandy and aromatic herbs. It tastes like gentian, mint, sage, apple, and vanilla.

The green variety tastes like absinthe and has 55% alcohol.

The yellow one has 40% alcohol, is milder and has sweeter herbal flavors.

Both varieties are an excellent digestif served chilled after dinner.

Génépi

It is a traditional liqueur made with herbs from the region of Savoie in the French Alps and Aosta in the Italian Alps. It tastes like absinthe. It is less sweet than many digestifs. It has a golden color.

Gentiane

It is a bittersweet, yellow liqueur made from the Massif Central. It also has accents of vanilla, candied orange, and spice.

Suze and Salers are famous brands. It is enjoyed as an aperitif over ice or just straight. It is quite a different taste.

A lot of people think French people are crazy to drink it because of the bitter taste. It was also used for medicinal purposes. My uncle Henri used to drink it for stomach problems!

NON-ALCOHOLIC DRINKS

Café au lait

As kids we had this almost every morning. This is hot coffee with hot milk. We would have a ¾ full bowl of milk and about ¼ of a bowl of hot coffee. My parents would have ¾ full bowl of hot coffee and about ¼ of a bowl of hot milk. So, you adjust the proportions as you grow older. The same principle as with the wine and water.

Hot chocolate

Hot chocolate is made with hot milk and a cocoa powder. As kids we used to drink Banania, a fortified hot chocolate, every morning. It was made of cocoa, banana flour, cereals, honey, and sugar. This drink was created in the beginning of the 20th century with the picture of a widely smiling Black man wearing a Fez. He is a Senegalese *tirailleur*, a French colonial infantry soldier. The image is controversial for the racial and colonial associations it creates. Not dissimilar to the debate over the images of Aunt Jemima and Uncle Ben used in United States.

The best hot chocolate you can have, is made with hot milk and melted chocolate at the Angelina tea house. It was founded in the 1900's at 226, Rue de Rivoli in Paris and now has many other locations. Parisians and tourists line up for their famous hot chocolate. Proust and Coco Chanel used to hang out in this place.

Lemonade and Orangeade

These are great for kids.

- 1 cup water
- 2 cups brown sugar
- 1 cup lemon or orange juice
- Mint leaves
- 3 cups cold water

Yields 1¾ quarts

Needed

- Saucepan
- Wooden spoon
- Strainer
- Pitcher

1) Make syrup by combining water and brown sugar in a saucepan and heat until it reaches a boil, and all the sugar is dissolved.
2) Add lemon juice or orange juice and a few leaves of mint. Let steep off heat for 15 minutes.
3) Strain syrup over a pitcher. Add cold water.
4) Refrigerate and enjoy drinking cold with ice cubes on a hot day.

It is very refreshing.

MINERAL WATERS

We drink these at any time of the day when we are thirsty, for lunch or after any exercise. It is good for the whole family every day because they are full of minerals.

Spring mineral waters abound all over Europe, in France there are over 80. These are the well-known brands.

Top naturally carbonated spring waters

Vichy Saint-Yorre and Vichy Célestins have bicarbonate. They are both Vichy water from the spring located in that town, also a spa, northeast of the Massif Central. Célestins eases the digestion after a big meal and helps the body to recuperate after a physical effort that caused heavy sweating. They are both mildly sparkling.

Badoit has less salt and is rich in magnesium, fluorine, and bicarbonates. It comes from a source in Saint Galmier in the Massif Central, west of the Rhône River. It is one of the most prestigious naturally carbonated mineral waters on the French tables. It is recommended for heartburns.

Vals spring water comes from a spring in Vals, west of the Rhône River, south of the volcanic land of the Massif Central. It has small bubbles and contains more calcium too.

Perrier carbonated water comes from a spring in Vergèze, near Nîmes in the south of France. It has bicarbonate, calcium, chloride, and other minerals but hardly any salt. It is perfect if you are on a low sodium diet. It comes in regular bubbles but also comes in small bubbles.

Top still mineral spring waters

Evian is full of mineral salt, rich in calcium and magnesium. Its spring is in Evian-les-Bains, in the northern part of the Alps, in Haute-Savoie, between the Mont Blanc and Lake Geneva. It is often used for babies and the whole family because it is slightly mineralized.

Contrex has sulfate, bicarbonate, and is rich in calcium and magnesium. Its spring is in Contrexéville, a spa in the Vosges region, in the northeast of France. It has hardly any sodium, so it is perfect for low sodium diets.

Vittel is also in the Vosges region, also a spa, next to Contrexéville. It contains mostly sulfate, bicarbonate and is rich in calcium. It will bring you ¼ of the calcium needed for an adult daily. It has hardly any sodium, so it is perfect for low sodium diets.

Volvic has a spring in the town of Volvic, right in the center of the volcanic chain of the Massif Central, at the foot of the *Puy de Dôme,* the highest extinct volcano in France. It has a volcanic basis, so it has silica, and very low sodium. It is good for the urinary track.

Seasonal Menu Ideas

Winter Lunch
- Salade de carottes râpées/Shredded Carrot Salad
- Pâté limousin/Limousin Pâté
- Fromages/Cheeses
- Bananes flambées/Flambéed bananas

Winter Dinner
- Omelette Parmentier/Potato Omelet
- Salade verte/Green Salad
- Fromage/Cheeses
- Flognarde

Spring Lunch
- Asperges sauce mousseline/Asparagus Mousseline sauce
- Boeuf bourguignon/Beef Burgundy
- Fromages/Cheeses
- Tarte aux fraises/Strawberry tart

Spring Dinner
- Soupe de légumes/Vegetable Soup
- Salade verte/Green salad
- Yaourt/Yogurt
- Cerises/Cherries

Summer Lunch

- ❖ Champignons à la grecque/Greek Style Mushrooms
- ❖ Tomates farcies/Stuffed Tomatoes
- ❖ Fromages/Cheeses
- ❖ Tartelettes aux framboises ou tarte aux abricots/ Raspberry tartlets or Apricot Tart

Summer Dinner

- ❖ Salade niçoise
- ❖ Fromages/Cheeses
- ❖ Crème renversée au caramel/Crème Caramel

Fall Lunch

- ❖ Soufflé au fromage/Cheese soufflé
- ❖ Poulet aux olives avec timbales de riz/Chicken with Olives and Molded Rice
- ❖ Mousse au chocolat/Chocolate Mousse

Fall Dinner

- ❖ Soupe aux girolles/Chanterelles Chowder
- ❖ Salade verte/Green Salad
- ❖ Yaourt/Yogurt
- ❖ Crêpes sucrées/Dessert crepes

Shopping for Food According to Mamie Gisèle

Of course, there are small and large supermarkets in France but my mom, Mamie Gisèle, did not like those *grandes surfaces* – large box stores, as opposed to my dad who enjoyed going there.

Whether you live in a big city, small town, little village, the outdoor markets in France are thriving—at last count over 10,000. It is a way to eat local and to eat better. There are open air markets and covered markets called *les Halles. Les Halles* are great in case of inclement weather. Most vendors are *maraîchers* – market gardeners. They sell their seasonal fresh fruits and vegetables. Many *maraîchers* will let you taste their fruit, but they do not want you to touch them. They will serve you. Mamie Gisèle liked to go to someone who would pick the fruit or vegetables that she pointed to, so at least she had a choice. She did not like when they were heavy handed and gave her more than she asked for!

Other vendors would be coming with their trucks and would be selling their meats, fish, cheeses, pastas. If you did not know how to prepare an item, the vendor would give you tips and recommendations.

Sometimes, you would see live animals being sold, like chicks, rabbits, chicken, or fish in tanks that you choose. In some markets you can also find vendors who sell shoes, fabrics, spices, antiques, CD's, records, candies and alike.

Most markets run on Fridays, Saturdays, or Sundays because people tend to shop more before the weekend. My mom used to keep track of *les jours de marché*, the outdoor market days, no matter what town or city she was in. <u>Marchedefrance.</u>

org will tell you the days outdoor markets run in French towns and cities. They typically run from 7:30 a.m. to 1:00 or 2:00 p.m. 2 to 3 times a week.

My mom's strategy was to go early and get the best pick of the seasonal produce at their peak of freshness, especially on hot days. She could also be back home in time to fix lunch, our main meal of the day. She was always conscious of time and did not like to go to places where the lines were too long. Often, before she left for the market, she did not have any idea of what she was going to fix for lunch. According to what she found seasonal and fresh at the market that day, she would plan her menu for lunch. When it was not a market day, she would still shop every day. She rarely froze meals. Fresh made was always her preference. She had to go to get the bread fresh at the boulangerie everyday anyway, so she might as well get other parts of the meal, right?

Another strategy was to go to the outdoor market at the end of the morning, when the market is going to close so you can get the best deals. Because a lot of vendors do not want to take back everything they brought with them you could get 2 kilograms of a produce for the price of 1 kilogram.

Not so serious shoppers or *flâneurs*, strollers, come around 10:00 or 10:30 a.m. when the entertainment is at its best. It could be music, dancing, a magician, or a parade advertising an upcoming event. Another strategy, if you have time, is to line up at the vendors where there is the longest line of local customers. This is usually a sign that the best merchandise is there. Patience is key and again arrive early!!

Often, the vendors have food for you to taste and if you have time to stroll through the market you can have well eaten by the time lunch rolls around. That would be my husband, Jean! Most vendors love to talk about their products.

In cities or towns that have a Saturday or Sunday market, there are vendors who cook in front of you, and you can take home a readymade meal!

When you go to the market, make sure you have one or two bags or like Mamie Gisèle, *une charrette*—a shopping cart, so when it becomes heavy, you pull it! Forget credit cards at the market! You better have cash!

For the tourists or *flâneurs*, after you are done visiting the market, you can stop at the café or bistro. This is a tradition in many cities, that my mom did not have time to experience. The café and bistro have a convivial atmosphere; you can have a coffee or a drink and use the restrooms. On market days, the cafés and bistros have a booming business between serving breakfast, midmorning goodies and lunch until midafternoon.

So, go to the outdoor markets, buy seasonal and plan your meal according to what you find that day!

At the French Table

French people take food and eating very seriously. It is an occasion to savor both food and the company of others. Lunch can take 45 minutes to 1 hour and it is usually served between 12:00 and 1:00 p.m.. Dinner can be as long and is served anytime between 7:00 p.m. and 9:00 p.m.. It takes time for good conversation and to properly savor the flavors of the food.

When seated at the table, your hands should be on the table as opposed to the Anglo- Saxon rule of keeping your hands off the table. The French tradition dates to Louis XIV court when the king was afraid that guests might put arsenic in his food or could have weapons hidden in their lap.

The table is typically set with a knife at the right of your plate and fork placed tines down on the left. When my parents visited the USA and we took them to a pizza or hamburger place, they were embarrassed to use their hands to eat and were always looking for silverware.

Wines are drunk with a meal and as children we drank water tinted with a little wine. The wine glass is placed on the top righthand side of the plate, with the water glass on the left of the wine glass. Soft drinks or milk are not served with a meal but are only drunk in between meals.

Your host will say *Bon appétit*, to signal that everyone can start eating. You are expected to stay seated during the whole meal. So, plan accordingly! Children must ask permission to leave the table and only then if they have finished eating.There are usually 4 to 5 courses, but portion sizes are small (appetizer, main course, maybe a green salad, cheese, and dessert). If there is a green salad, usually you do not cut it with a knife. You can fold it with the help of your knife onto your fork.

If a cheese has been wrapped in paper like for a Camembert or a Brie, you can eat the rind, do not cut it off! If it is a hard cheese like a Comté, Gruyère, Petit Basque, with a hard rind, please cut it off!

Do not spread foie gras or creamy cheese evenly across your bread like butter. It should sit on top of the bread as a *cavalier* and eaten and savored as is.

If you are a guest, it is not polite to serve yourself wine or water. The host will serve you and top your glass. If you are a woman, you should not grab the bottle and serve yourself.

A piece of bread is put on the table on the left side of your plate. There is no bread plate or butter for the bread. You can break off small pieces with your hand to put in your mouth. At home it is ok to mop up juices with your bread. If you put a baguette or a loaf of bread on the table, it should not be turned upside down since it is bad luck.

If there is one last piece of food left, pass it to someone else and if they refuse, you might take it. Asking for more does not exist.

My husband Jean, me, our daughter Natacha and her husband Craig, in my cousins' restaurant in the Limousin region, *La ferme auberge des Ruchers des Bruyères*

Tips and Hacks
Astuces et trucs

In our family kitchen, there are some tips and hacks, known or less known that are passed from generation to generation. This list is not exhaustive so here are a few:

- We usually cook with butter and oil in a frying pan. Why? The butter prevents the oil from spattering and the oil prevents the butter from burning.
- To prevent your salt to stick in the saltshaker, put a few grains of rice
- If a dish you made is too salty, add one sliced potato to absorb the salt or you can add a tablespoon of crème fraiche.
- If you want to cool wine faster, add salt to the ice bucket.
- To give your puff pastry a golden, professional look brush the outside of it with a mixture of 1 egg yolk with a tablespoon of milk.
- To make a professional glaze on a fruit tart combine jam or jelly with rum or Grand Marnier to taste. When liquefied, apply with a brush on the fruit. The glaze will solidify as it cools and give a brilliant look to the tart.
- If your crepe batter has lumps, use an immersion blender, and beat at high speed and the lumps should be gone. Another tip is to strain the batter with a strainer or a chinois.
- To blanch green vegetables that you want to stay green (green beans, asparagus, broccoli), salt the water, do not cover your pot and after 3-5 minutes plunge the vegetables in ice water.
- When cooking rice or noodles, this is how we measure in most French families: one handful per person and one for the saucepan.
- Keep parsley, chives, chervil, oregano, thyme, and other herbs fresh in a glass of water for a few weeks, and to prevent the water from stagnating, add a piece of a charcoal briquet in the water. That works for flowers too.
- To keep leftover minced garlic, shallots, or onions, place it in a little bowl and keep covered with olive oil in the refrigerator.
- Very often in France, we keep hard boiled eggs in the fridge. To know if your eggs in the fridge are cooked or raw, spin them. If it spins easily, it is a hardboiled. If it has a hard time spinning it is raw.
- Store onions and potatoes separately! Onions produce ethylene gas that speed up the ripening process so when they are together potatoes will rot.
- Tomatoes and cucumbers should be stored at room temperature. They do not do well in the fridge where their texture is altered.
- And finally, if you wonder whether your freezer lost power during your

absence, freeze a glass of water before you leave and place a coin on top of the frozen water. If when you come back, the coin is at the bottom of the glass your freezer lost power and food may have spoiled.

Acknowledgements

Cooking has been a family affair for a long time, from my parents to our daughter. I want to thank my daughter Natacha for her patience with me, especially during holiday meal preparations when she was in her teenage years. I am sure it was not easy since we both like things done right. Talk about a labor of love! She helped me become a better cook! Nowadays, she keeps me challenged every day in cooking. She has surpassed me by a long shot, making bread and croissants from scratch. I am just amazed and proud of all the special dishes she prepares! She is on her way.

Her husband, Craig is the master of barbecue. Thanks to him, I have learned about slow cooking barbecue, rubs, barbecue sauces and venison cooking. Both are avid foodies! It is a delight to cook for them and to share meals with them.

Even though I cook mostly French, I have learned from Maxine Kopczynski, our American mom, regarding the preparation of Thanksgiving meals and other American traditional dishes. Thank you, Maxine, for teaching me, American family cooking!

In our American family, we have some great cooks. Michael Moore, my American brother-in-law, challenges me all the time and I enjoy cooking with him. He is organized, adventuresome and enjoys exploring all cuisines. He is a fearless cook indoors and out and the best editor I have ever met.

I consider myself highly qualified in the kitchen, but writing a book was a whole new challenge. In addition to Michael's editorial guidance, his wife Elizabeth

Kopczynski-Moore is an expert proofreader, and I am grateful for her help sharpening my English grammar, punctuation, and syntax. Beth Daniels' proofing late in the project provided the always valuable insights of a pair of fresh eyes. Michael and Elizabeth, my Cliffview Media team, you helped me get this book out of the starting blocks and across the finish line. You are truly jewels!

Maxine, our American mother and matriarch

In my French family, I would like to thank my brother, Pascal Martinie, and his wife Fabienne, from beautiful Bretagne -- Brittany. They are supporting my passion by sending me ideas of new Breton dishes and Breton cookbooks or even sending food. They are gourmets and gourmands! Pascal is also quite talented in technology and has developed videos of my cooking classes. He also helped me reminiscing family stories tied to food. His advice has been priceless.

Mamie Gisèle, brother Pascal, me and a friend in the Limousin region

I want to acknowledge the Alliance Française of Portland for allowing me to give cooking classes on the regions of France from my kitchen. Thank you, Sherry, Elene, and Don, for your support and flexibility with our crazy schedules.

I want to thank all my neighbors also, for being my guinea pigs, helping me taste many recipes. You are all good sports: Pat, Tim, David, Carolyn, Holden, Miles, Cadence, Arlin, Linda, Nitin and Niha. I am also grateful for all my friends, too many to mention--you know who you are, who helped me sample my various dishes.

I am so appreciative to have met Kary Arimoto-Mercer, in the '80s and collaborated on recipes for our East meets West cooking classes, using similar ingredients found both in Asian and French cuisine.

I am fortunate to have had amazing recipe testers: Chris Bell, Natacha Chough, Annette Dincelli, Monica Grinnell, Martha Hamil, Katharine Jensen, Judy Kafoury, Sausha Knott, Laura Kretschmar, Rhonda Lynn, Kary Arimoto-Mercer, Kathryn Moore, Chloé Moore, Michael Moore, Sue Richmond, Sherri Roberts, Anne Santa, John Santa, Karen Tindall, Daniel Wilson, Liz Zacca and Elene Zedginidze. These recipes could not have been foolproof if everyone, beside me, did not try them. Thank you for helping me test recipes in your kitchen and giving me detailed feedback. This was a Roman task. Your guidance was very much appreciated.

I have departed family members and friends that I want to recognize and thank for helping me become a more diverse cook. My parents René and Gisèle, whom I watched cooking while growing up have been a great influence. I have collected their recipe cards and books over the years. I miss them both tremendously. They both enjoyed food either at home or on various excursions!

My mom and dad also known as Mamie Gisèle and Papy René in their garden

Margaret Kretschmar introduced me to Ukrainian foods and Scottish Haggis. It was a treat to make Holubtsi cabbage rolls and celebrate the Ukrainian New Year with all our friends! She would also have a party on January 25th to celebrate the famous Scottish poet, Robert Burns birthday with Haggis, ground lamb meat cooked in a lamb lung or stomach! Lo and behold, I found out that lamb lungs were not allowed to be sold in the USA since 1971! These were great occasions for Margaret to prolong the holiday season throughout January and have another party. For me, it was another reason to learn about other cultures through their cuisine.

Mamie Gisèle with my husband Jean
in her kitchen

Eleanor Van Tilburg and her husband Wayne were quite the Francophiles and always ready to collaborate with me and organize Christmas parties with themes from different countries—one year British, one year Danish, one year French and so on. How fun it was to plan the menus and cook at their house. Their house was Party Central as Eleanor used to call it!

My late mother-in-law and her sister have stretched my skills in Korean cooking. Thanks to them and their guidance, I was able to fix all kinds of authentic Korean family delicacies for family and friends.

Consuelo Casey, of Filipino origins and from Hawaii, our daughter's godmother, was a wiz at Asian cooking. She cooked by feel so I really had to pay attention. I learned a lot from her.

The biggest acknowledgement of all goes to my husband, Jean, an adventurous eater, and gourmet food lover, which is what you want for a food taster, right? He has been tasting all my recipes, putting up with my attention to details, my stressing out about perfecting dishes, cleaning up after me, doing the dishes, and everything else that made me unlovable, but his reward was knowing there had to be a good meal to eat in the end! Thank you for being so patient and for being a good sport!

My parents family home and garden

Made in the USA
Monee, IL
04 May 2024

57877597R10157